Project and Program
RISK MANAGEMENT
A Guide to Managing Project
Risks and Opportunities

Edited By:
R. Max Wideman
Fellow, PMI

A Publication of the Project Management Institute
14 Campus Boulevard
Newtown Square, Pennsylvania 19073 USA
610/356-4600 Fax: 610/356-4647
E-mail: customercare@pmi.org
Web: www.PMI.org/Marketplace

Library of Congress Cataloging-in-Publication Data

Edited by: Wideman, R. Max.
     Project and program risk management: a guide to managing project risks
     and opportunities/R. Max Wideman
          p.   cm .—(The PMBOK handbook series: v.no.6)
          Includes bibliographical references.
     ISBN 1-880410-00-1 (10 vol. set).—ISBN 1-880410-06-0 (vol.6)
     1. Industrial project management.   2. Risk management.   I. Title.   II. Series.
HD69.P76W54 1992
658.4'04–dc20

                                                92-3336
                                               CIP

ISBN 13: 978-1-880410-06-6
ISBN 10: 1-880410-06-0 (Volume 6)
          1-880410-00-1 (10 Volume Set)

Published by: Project Management Institute, Inc.
                             14 Campus Boulevard
                             Newtown Square, Pennsylvania 19073-3299 USA
                             Phone: +1-610-356-4600
                             Fax: +1-610-356-4647
                             E-mail: customercare@pmi.org
                             Internet: www.PMI.org

PMI Publications welcomes corrections and comments on its books. Please feel free to send comments on
typographical, formatting, or other errors. Simply make a copy of the relevant page of the book, mark the
error, and send it to: Book Editor, PMI Publications, 14 Campus Boulevard, Newtown Square, PA 19073-
3299 USA.

To inquire about discounts for resale or educational purposes, please contact the PMI Book Service
Center.
PMI Book Service Center
P.O. Box 932683, Atlanta, GA 31193-2683 USA
Phone: 1-866-276-4764 (within the U.S. or Canada) or +1-770-280-4129 (globally)
Fax: +1-770-280-4113
E-mail: book.orders@pmi.org

The paper used in this book complies with the Permanent Paper Standard issued by the National
Information Standards Organization (Z39.48—1984).

20 19 18 17 16

Foreword

This publication is the second in a series of nine handbooks developed by the Project Management Institute (PMI). The series is designed to complement the Project Management Body of Knowledge (PMBOK) as codified by PMI.

This handbook deals with the function of Risk Management in the context of project or program management. It establishes the need for examining risks and opportunities in project work and describes approaches which can lead to significant reduction of the risks as well as to better project performance. This is a sometimes overlooked aspect of project management which can often result in significant improvements in the ultimate success of the project.

This handbook should appeal equally to those who are looking for a summary of the basics of project and program risk management, as well as to those who are studying for PMI's certification program. In addition, the material in the handbook will benefit course developers, trainers and academics who are seeking guidance as to appropriate project and program risk management educational content.

In keeping with previous practice, this first printing of the handbook is being made available as a "Preliminary Issue for Trial Use and Comment." Since the content is tied specifically to the PMBOK, it is important to ensure that PMI members support the material and its manner of presentation. I hope, therefore, that readers will take a moment to contribute constructive suggestions for improving and upgrading the next issue by completing and returning the Comments page at the end of this book.

The material in this handbook has been assembled entirely by voluntary PMI member effort and, as anyone knows who has been involved in similar undertakings, requires many hours of dedicated effort. In particular I would like to acknowledge the efforts of Max Wideman and the many people who provided comments and suggestions on the various drafts. To all those who contributed their thoughts and writings to this first issue, I express our appreciation for a job well done!

Rodney J. Dawson
President, Project Management Institute

Preface

Welcome to project and program risk management!

In a very real sense, progress is made by spotting opportunities and taking advantage of them. Once identified, the most aggressive way of taking advantage of such opportunities is by establishing a *project*. Thus, the whole point of a project is to introduce some change which will be beneficial in financial or other ways to the sponsors and users of the project.

However, introducing change means introducing something new, to venture forth, to take some risks. So *risks* are the corollary of opportunity. They represent exposure to mischance, hazards, and the possibility of adverse consequences. They are the down-side of a project undertaking. While project management is the best way of managing opportunity, taking risks has always been a fundamental part of the process, and this needs to be pro-actively managed through the function of Project and Program Risk Management.

Generally, when we speak of taking a risk we tend to think of those things which are at long odds, are highly chancy and possibly hazardous. Yet many risks we take in everyday life are so commonplace that we scarcely give them a thought. Instead, we treat them as mere uncertainties and react to them subconsciously, taking precautions that experience has taught us are only prudent.

However, in today's markets with more difficult economic conditions, tougher competition, and ever advancing technology, project uncertainty and risk have assumed significantly greater proportions. Indeed, in most projects, not only are the uncertainties and risks numerous, but they are also interrelated. This affects project results in complex ways, making it difficult for management to be confident in forecasting the final results.

Therefore, Project and Program Risk Management is seen as the formal process whereby the risks and opportunities are systematically identified, assessed and appropriately provided for in the course of project planning and implementation. It means taking a pro-active stance to cultivate an environment in which project and program risks are significantly reduced, if not eliminated entirely, and opportunities are cultivated. Project and Program Risk Management should encompass the full spectrum of activities associated with the handling of project uncertainties.

As one of project management's integrative functions (see PMBOK Handbook Volume 1, *A Framework for Project and Program Management Integration*) Project and Program Risk Management is inextricably tied into each of the other project management functions, especially the four basic project constraints of Scope, Quality, Time and Cost. It is, therefore, a key function of the project management process. However, management's attitude towards risk, in many cases, is governed by the extent of their understanding of the risk management process, their confidence in the associated techniques and in the analytical results obtained. Others consider the subject too mathematical, yet many risks relate to people and their attitudes. Hence the need for this handbook.

Acknowledgments

Understandably, the risks associated with large and very large projects have received noteworthy attention in the literature, because of the substantial sums of money involved on the one hand, and the political and professional reputations of the sponsors on the other. On lesser projects, however, aspects of the project which may be at risk are frequently submerged in an all-encompassing "contingency allowance" determined as a result of some previous experience. For many, this approach may be quite satisfactory, yet closer examination of the subject indicates that including risk as a pro-active management function provides project management with an added management opportunity.

Project and Program Risk Management furnishes the chance to better understand the nature of the project at hand, to involve team members in its strengths and weaknesses, and generally to integrate the core functions of Scope, Quality, Time and Cost with the interactive functions of Human Resources, Contract/Procurement, and Information/Communications management. For these reasons, PMI early recognized the importance of this subject to the overall success of a project, no matter what its size or area of application, and so identified Project and Program Risk Management as a separate PMBOK topic.

Once again many PMI members, too numerous to cite all by name, have enthusiastically volunteered material, suggestions and encouragement for the development of this handbook. I would, however, like to mention a few who have been particular contributors or my mentors in this effort: Mike Curran, David Hamburger, and Bill Hosley for most helpful explanations, conversations and text; David Hulett for a copy of an excellent Orange County Chapter workshop handout on Risk Management; Pat Buckley and Bill Duncan for a change in emphasis; Chris Quaife for both written contributions and thorough and perceptive comments on my original texts; and Davidson Frame for encouragement and testing the handbook in one of his classes. I am sure that readers will benefit greatly from their work. Any errors of interpretation or omissions are, of course, my own responsibility.

As always, my wife Audrey has been most supportive of this work and patiently endured through many hours of moans and groans arising from the effort of putting pen to paper (or more contemporarily, fingers to keyboard).

R. Max Wideman, Fellow, PMI
Editor

Contents

Appendices

A. Typical Project Risks

B. Impact Analysis Methodology

C. Other Risk Analysis Techniques

D. Risk Applied to Schedule and Cost

E. A Glossary of Project and Program Risk Management Terminology

Illustrations

Chapter I Introduction

A. Handbook Purpose and Content

The purpose of this handbook is to provide a simplified understanding of the nature of project risk and opportunity, and a systematic approach to risk reduction. For brevity and ease of reference, it is deliberately structured in simple and concise terms, often in bullet format, or by graphic illustrations.

This handbook is one of a family of nine, designed to provide a summary level review of each of the major functional areas of project management. These functional areas are those codified in the Project Management Institute's Project Management Body of Knowledge (PMBOK). This handbook provides a useful insight into the process of project risk management for anyone contemplating a project, whether it is a small administrative project, a large capital works project, or anything in between. It also provides an introduction for those intending to study for PMI's Project Management Professional (PMP) certification exam.

B. Why Project Risk Management?

Corporate management has the responsibility to make formal judgments and appropriate decisions that will lead the organization to a successful destiny. Ideally, such decisions should be taken in an environment of *total certainty*, wherein all the necessary information is available for making the right decision, and the outcome can be predicted with a high degree of confidence. In reality, most decisions are taken without complete information, and therefore give rise to some degree of *uncertainty* in the outcome. In the extreme case of complete absence of information, nothing is known about the outcome and *total uncertainty* prevails.

Organizational survival in today's world is achieved by pursuing *opportunity* within this spectrum of uncertainty and projects are typically launched to take advantage of these opportunities. Thus, the whole point of undertaking a project is to achieve or establish something new, to venture, to take chances, so risk has always been an intrinsic part of project work. However, in today's markets, with heavy competition, advanced technology and tough economic conditions, risk taking has assumed significantly greater proportions.

The goals of risk management, therefore, are to identify project risks and develop strategies which either significantly reduce them or take steps to avoid them altogether. At the same time, steps should be taken to maximize associated opportunities. In essence, it involves planning which minimizes the probability and net effects of things going wrong, and carefully matches responsibility to residual risks which are unavoidably retained. It is a very constructive and creative process.

As a simple example, one way of avoiding a possible traffic jam while driving on the highway to a particular destination is to consider alternative forms of transportation. Granted that each may have its own particular set of risks, but careful comparison should identify the best set of alternatives with the lowest overall degree of uncertainty or risk of arriving late. However, the impact of each on the time and cost of the journey must also be taken into account if the best overall arrangement for a successful arrival is to be achieved. The selection may well depend on the relative priorities given to the cost, schedule, and quality of the journey! If the real objective of the exercise is to hold a meeting, then perhaps the opportunity could be taken to hold the meeting at a more favorable intermediate location?

In short, the purpose of project risk management is to:

- Specifically identify factors that are likely to impact the project objectives of Scope, Quality, Time and Cost
- Quantify the likely impact of each factor
- Give a baseline for Project Noncontrollables
- Mitigate impacts by exercising influence over Project Controllables

The scope for project risk management lies somewhere between the two extremes of total certainty and total uncertainty, as shown in Figure I.1.

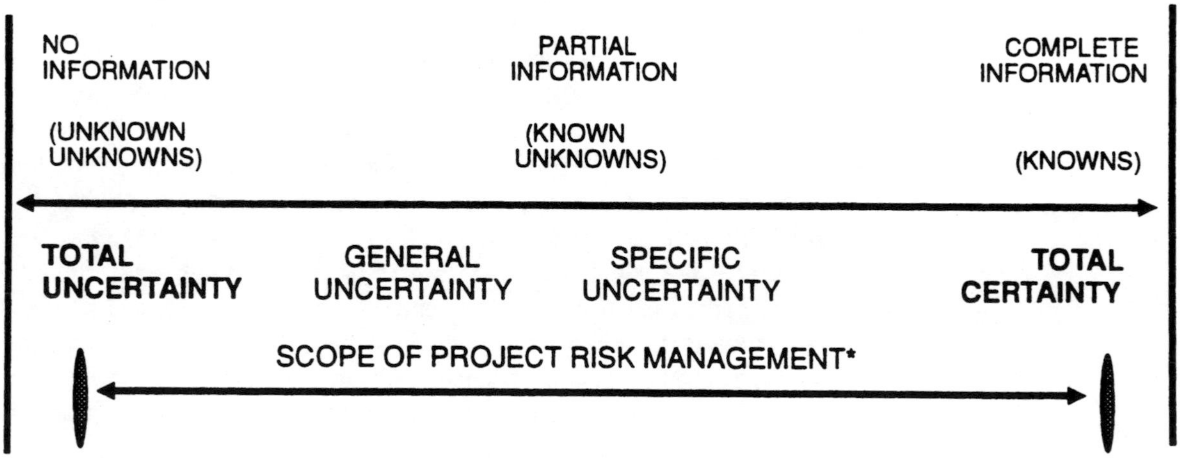

*Note: In this range the information to be sought is known

Figure I.1 The Uncertainty Spectrum

C. Uncertainty, Opportunity and Risk

From the foregoing it will be seen that uncertainty, opportunity and risk are closely allied. It can be visualized that unknowns about the future may turn out to be either favorable or unfavorable, but *lack of knowledge of future events* constitutes *uncertainty* so that uncertainty is simply the set of all possible outcomes, both favorable and unfavorable. In this relationship, the probability of those outcomes which are favorable may be viewed as *opportunity*, while the probability of those outcomes which are unfavorable represent *risk*.[1]

Similarly, most opportunities when pursued carry with them associated risks and, generally speaking, the greater the opportunity, the greater is the degree of uncertainty and the consequent associated risk. Thus, opportunity and risk are also tied together and, indeed, one may be seen as the corollary of the other. This relationship is shown diagrammatically in Figure I.2.

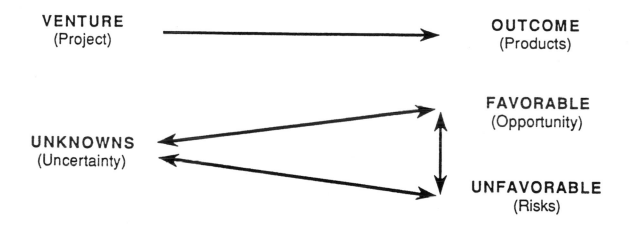

THE GOAL: Project Risk Management's function is to move uncertainty away from risk and towards opportunity

Figure I.2. The Uncertainty/Opportunity/Risk Relationship

In the context of project management *Project Risk* is defined as follows:

Project Risk is the cumulative effect of the chances of uncertain occurrences adversely affecting project objectives.

In other words, it is the degree of exposure to negative events, and their probable consequences impacting on project objectives, as expressed in terms of scope, quality, time and cost.[2]

However, just as risks are associated with pursuing opportunities, so opportunities also flow from encountering risks. Indeed, many a risk which occurs in the event can, with a little foresight and ingenuity, be turned into an opportunity! Unfortunately, all too often risks are either ignored or dealt with in a very arbitrary way so that such opportunities are overlooked.

The constant goal of project risk management should be to move uncertainty away from risk and towards opportunity. Consequently, when assessing overall impacts of uncertainty on a project, it is the net project risk which should be determined, i.e., the cumulative net effect of the chances of both adverse and favorable consequences affecting project objectives.

D. The Nature of Risk Management

Generally, when we speak of taking a risk we tend to think only of those things which are highly chancy or hazardous. Yet many risks are so commonplace in everyday life that we scarcely give them a thought. Instead, we react to them subconsciously, and take precautions that experience has taught us are only prudent.

In crossing the road, we take the precaution of looking both ways and only cross when the road is clear. If we are in a hurry, we might "take a chance" (increase the risk) by crossing when we see a sufficient gap in the traffic. If the traffic is heavy, and the risk appears to be extreme, then we might walk further to a designated crossing area at an intersection with traffic lights, or even to a safer overpass, if there is one (risk reduced by trading off time and energy).

Rarely do we systematically identify all the risks involved in reaching our destination. Even less do we consider the consequences should our chances fail to come off except, perhaps, once a serious accident has actually occurred. Otherwise, we might decide never to go anywhere at all!

When it comes to our own family, however, we are inclined to take an entirely different approach. After all, we are now dealing with something very precious and with a lot of potential.

When our children are small, we admonish them not to go near the road (risk identification and avoidance). When they must cross the road, say, to get to school, we examine the dangers and either teach them how to cross safely or direct them to the school crossing guard (risk assessment and planning or shift of responsibility). When they get home at the end of the day, we ask them "how they got on"?—perhaps we can do something more to help them for tomorrow (information feedback and corrective action). We also make a mental note for when our youngest reaches the same age (building the data base). Thus, we have established the basic elements of managing project risk.

E. Project Risk Management is Pro-active

Project managers will recognize the classic systems methodology outlined in the previous section. This consists of *input*, *process*, *output* and *feedback loop*, a basic model which is so vital to the effective control of any project. Yet risk is somehow different. It has to do with uncertainty, probability or unpredictability, and contingent planning.

Indeed, the term *Project Risk Management* itself tends to be misleading because management implies complete control of events. On the contrary, project risk management should be seen as advanced preparation for possible adverse future events, rather than responding as they happen. With such advanced planning it should be possible to select an alternative action plan which will still enable project objectives to be achieved successfully.

Consider this improbable, but quite possible, situation. You are at risk of being shot at. You have four options.

Reactive:
1. You can move to avoid the bullet;
2. You can deflect the bullet; or
3. You can repair the damage done by the bullet.

Pro-active:
4. You can take steps to avoid being confronted by the person with the gun.

Crisis management (reactive mode) consists of selecting the appropriate response. However, if anticipation and planning make it possible to avoid the situation in the first place (pro-active mode) then this approach would obviously be better. Unless, of course, there are compelling reasons to the contrary such as conducting a controversial political campaign! The point is: *at no time are you in control of the bullet* (the risk event).[3]

F. Risk and Decision Makers

A risk should only be taken when the potential benefit and chances of winning exceed the remedial cost of an unsuccessful decision and chances of losing by a satisfactory margin. Therefore, the risk taker should obtain realistic answers to questions such as:[4]

- Why should the risk be taken?
- What will be gained?
- What could be lost?
- What are the chances of success (and failure)?
- What can be done if the desired result is not achieved?
- Is the potential reward worth the risk?

Risk elements that tend to attract and/or determine the response attitudes of decision makers include:[5]

- Potential frequency of loss
- Amount and reliability of information available
- Potential severity of loss
- Manageability of the risk
- Vividness of the consequences
- Potential for (adverse) publicity
- Ability to measure the consequences
- Whose money is it

Severity of the potential loss appears to attract the most attention because individuals appear to be willing to accept small (even frequent) losses, but are averse to a risk which has high stakes. Even so, a major thrust must be to minimize unwarranted optimism, prejudice, ignorance or self-interest. Good ways to do this include responding to the following issues:[6]

- Has it been done before?
- How close is the analogy?

    and

- Seek out corroborative evidence.
- Get personal interviews with those with the experience.
- Obtain alternative opinions.
- Insist on written assessments, quantitative if possible.

Avoid creating additional risk by rushing, understaffing, underfunding, or ignoring the obvious. Simply try to adopt well-established good project management practices, and so escape the well-known adage: "There's never enough time to do it right the first time, but time enough to do it over if its wrong!"

But sooner or later a decision has to be made. Never lose sight of the basic reason for taking a risk—to gain a specific reward. Some typical project rewards (or benefits) include:

- Achieving a desired result using limited resources,
- Advancing the state-of-the-art,
- Meeting a required end date or improving a schedule,
- Enhancing profitability,
- Increasing a budget or schedule contingency,
- Saving money or offsetting a fiscal variance,
- Improving the firm's market position, or
- Ensuring customer satisfaction.

In each case, the potential reward must be accurately defined and, if at all possible, measured in common terms such as cost. If a finite dollar value cannot be assigned to a particular outcome (e.g., customer satisfaction), it may be necessary to assign an arbitrary value to the intangible benefit for purposes of risk/reward evaluation. This may be far more difficult than it seems as marketing's valuation of customer satisfaction, for example, will generally exceed a judgment made by manufacturing or engineering. Decision makers who use information from various sources in evaluating the risk must temper their biased judgments to ensure objectivity in the risk assessment process.[7] So:[8]

- Make the best decision given the state of knowledge—even so, it may not work out.
- Distinguish between a good decision and a good outcome.
- Since it is not possible to be certain of a good outcome, increase the probability of good outcomes by making good decisions!

Here are some helpful rules-of-thumb for the project manager.[9] Don't take the risk if:

- The organization cannot afford to lose;
- The exposure to the outcome is too great;
- The situation (or the project) is just not worth it;
- The odds are not in the project's favor;
- It is no more than a "fair bet";
- The benefits are not identified;
- There appear to be a large number of acceptable alternatives
    (The greater the number, the more the uncertainty.);
- The risk does not achieve a project objective;
- The expected value from the baseline assumptions is negative or is negative with small changes in assumptions;
- The data is unorganized, without structure or pattern;
- There is not enough data to compute the results
    (Get more data or do research.);
- A contingency plan for recovery is not in place should the results prove to be less than satisfactory.

1. Construction Industry Institute, Management of Project Risks and Uncertainties, The University of Texas at Austin, October 1989.
2. *PMBOK*, 3/28/87, p E-2.
3. D.C. Fraser, Risk Minimisation in Giant Projects, International Conference on the Successful Accomplishment of Giant Projects, London, England, May 1978.
4. D. Hamburger, The Project Manager: Risk Taker and Contingency Planner, *PMJ*, June 1990, p44.
5. Construction Industry Institute, Management of Project Risks and Uncertainties, The University of Texas at Austin, October 1989, p3-4.
6. J.N. Brooke, Leveraged Risk Reduction, *Proceedings PMI Seminar/Symposium*, Atlanta, Georgia 1989, p302.
7. D. Hamburger, The Project Manager: Risk Taker and Contingency Planner, *PMJ*, June 1990, p45.
8. D.T. Hulett, PMP Certification Workshop - Risk Management, PMI Orange County Chapter, 1991, p12.
9. Ibid., p1 and p58.

Chapter II   Integration, General Approach and Definition

A. Integrating Risk into Project Management

Experience on many projects reveals poor performance in terms of reaching scope, quality, time and cost objectives. Many of these shortcomings are attributed either to unforeseen events, which might or might not have been anticipated by more experienced project management, or to foreseen events for which the risks were not fully accommodated.

Perhaps one of the biggest hurdles is that of management's attitude to risk itself. Some have little understanding of the concepts, while others lack confidence in the mathematical techniques and results obtained, preferring to rely alternatively on aggressive risk taking or undue caution. Or again, inherent risks may simply be optimistically ignored. In reality, far better decisions with higher chances of project success are reached by facing these issues. For some project managers this may represent a new working environment.

Figure II.1 shows schematically how the function of project risk management is inextricably tied into the remaining seven PMBOK management functions. Note how specific areas of risk are associated with each of the individual functions as shown on the diagram. Each should be carefully evaluated as part of the risk management responsibility.

A long list of potential project risks is provided in Appendix A. Not all of these risks apply to all projects, of course, but many do, and failure to manage risk in the manner described in the following chapters can lead to significant and unnecessary losses. Poor past track records should be significantly improved by a generally better understanding and application of the project risk management function.

B. The Natural Project Risk Management Sequence

The greatest degree of uncertainty about the future is encountered in the concept phase of a project. Directions taken by the project sponsors in this phase have the greatest influence on the ultimate scope, quality, time and cost of the project. Also, change is an inevitable part of the iterative nature of managing projects, yet its extent and effects are often under-estimated at this time. Therefore, the need for a process for the realistic appraisal of factors affecting the accomplishment phases of the project is essential.

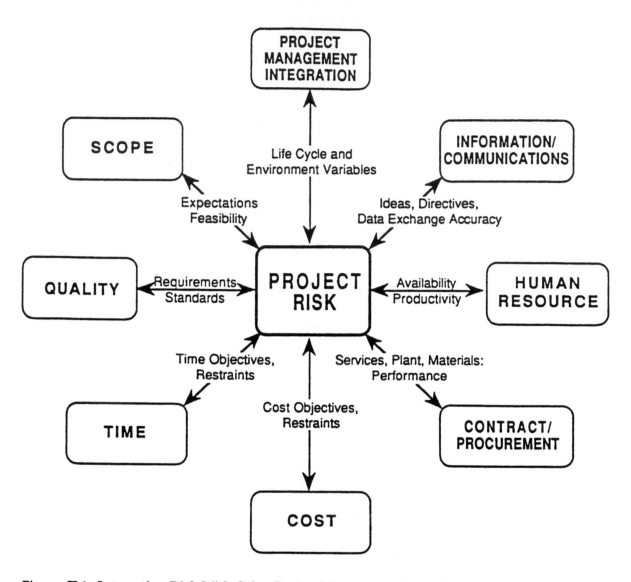

Figure II.1. Integrating Risk With Other Project Management Functions
After C. Quaife, 1/11/90

Project Risk Management is seen as a formal process whereby risks are systematically identified, assessed and provided for. In other words, this function involves a deliberate sequence of *identification* followed by *mitigation*. The latter calls for both assessment and response, which may include such defensive actions as *risk avoidance* or *deflection* by allocating appropriate risks to insurers or by other contractual arrangements; a careful *risk assessment* or detailed *impact analysis; response planning* and *contingency planning,* such as the development of alternative *workarounds* (discussed in Chapter VI.B); and the provision and prudent management of a budgeted *contingency allowance.*

Not only are the uncertainties in most projects numerous, but they may also be interrelated. This affects project results in complex ways. It tends to lead to under-estimation of risk which makes it difficult for management to be confident in identifying and prioritizing the areas on which risk management should be focused. A systematic approach is required to sort through the myriad of uncertainties, to pinpoint the truly critical ones, and to identify effective ways of reducing those uncertainties, consistent with overall project objectives.

In practice, depending on the size and nature of the project, effective risk management may require some quite detailed quantitative assessment of the impacts of the various uncertainties. This data provides a basis for judging the reliability of the original estimates, the effectiveness of possible alternative strategies, and for planning the best overall responses.

C. Risk Management - An Integrative Function

As noted in Section A, failure to give proper recognition to risk management on a project can lead to unnecessary and often substantial losses, or even complete project failure. The status of risk on a project varies significantly during the course of its life cycle, and, as with most of the other project functions, the most effective time for achieving the greatest impact on project results is early on in the project development phase. Consequently, risk management should be established as a continuing integrative function throughout the project's life cycle.

Figure II.1 illustrated schematically how risk management integrates with each of the other project management functions, and Table II.1 provides further examples of how some typical risk events (defined in Chapter III.F) can surface in any one of these functional areas.[1] In the groupings tabulated, risk items are associated with the headings in which the impact is most direct. For example, poor organization is an indirect risk (threat) to Quality, but is shown under Human Resources, which it affects directly. Note that "contractor" is used in the broadest sense of anyone, including an employee, who undertakes to perform any work or service at a price, salary or wage.

D. Project Risk Management Definition

This leads to the definition of Project Risk Management as follows:[2]

Project Risk Management is the art and science of identifying, assessing and responding to project risk throughout the life of a project and in the best interests of its objectives.

Figures III.1 and III.2 in Chapter III show a Risk Management breakdown structure following the typical hierarchy of PMI's Body of Knowledge Management Functions. That is to say the function itself is level 1, followed successively by *processes, activities,* and finally *techniques* at level 4. As illustrated earlier, and as shown in the figures, the Risk Management processes are Risk Identification; Risk Deflection (Insurable), Impact Risk Assessment; Response Planning; the Response System; and the Application of the resulting Data.

Chapter II   Integration, General Approach and
Definition

Table II.1. Typical Functional Distribution of Controllable Risk Items

PM Integration
Risk Events
- Incorrect start of integrated PM relative to project life cycle

Risk Conditions
- Inadequate planning, integration or resource allocation (Anything which reduces the probability of properly determining project objectives, i.e., anything which directly or indirectly reduces the probability of project success.)
- Inadequate, or lack of post-project review

Scope
Risk Events
- Changes in scope to meet project objectives, e.g., regulatory changes

Risk Conditions
- Inadequacy of planning, or planning lead time
- Poor definition of scope breakdown, or work packages
- Inconsistent, incomplete or unclear definition of quality requirements
- Inadequate scope control during implementation

Quality
Risk Events
- Performance failure, or environmental impact

Risk Conditions
- Poor attitude to quality
- Substandard design/materials/ workmanship
- Inadequate quality assurance program

Time
Risk Events
- Specific delays, e.g., strikes, labor or material availability, extreme weather, rejection of work

Risk Conditions
- Errors in estimating time or resource availability
- Poor allocation and management of float
- Scope of work changes without due allowance for time extensions/acceleration
- Early release of competitive product

Cost
Risk Events
- Impacts of accidents, fire, theft
- Unpredictable price changes, e.g., due to supply shortages

Risk Conditions
- Estimating errors, including estimating uncertainty
- Lack of investigation of predictable problems
- Inadequate productivity, cost, change or contingency control
- Poor maintenance, security, purchasing, etc.

Risk
Risk Events
- The risk of overlooking a risk
- Changes in the work necessary to achieve the scope

Risk Conditions
- Ignoring risk or "assuming it away"
- Inappropriate or unclear assignment of responsibility/ risk to employees/contractors
- Poor insurance management
- Inappropriate or unclear contractual assignment of risk

Contract/Procurement
Risk Events
- Contractor insolvency
- Claims settlement or litigation

Risk Conditions
- Unenforceable conditions/clauses
- Incompetent or financially unsound workers/contractors
- Adversarial relations
- Inappropriate or unclear contractual assignment of risk

Human Resources
Risk Events
- Strikes, terminations, organizational breakdown

Risk Conditions
- Conflict not managed
- Poor organization, definition or allocation of responsibility, or otherwise absence of motivation
- Poor use of accountability
- Absence of leadership, or vacillating management style
- Consequences of ignoring or avoiding risk

Communications
Risk Events
- Inaction or wrong action due to incorrect information or communication failure

Risk Conditions
- Carelessness in planning or in communicating
- Improper handling of complexity
- Lack of adequate consultation with project's "publics" (internal/external)

E. Variation of Risk Factors Through the Project Life Cycle

As anyone who has been associated with any sizeable project well knows, the life cycle of a project is very dynamic, i.e., characterized by rapid change. It should not come as a surprise to learn that the project risk factors are also subject to considerable change during the project life cycle. The nature of this project life cycle and some of its special characteristics are discussed in detail in PMBOK Handbook Volume 1, *A Framework for Project and Program Management Integration.*

For purposes of this handbook, it is worth noting that a typical project is made up of four generic phases, consisting of *concept, development, implementation,* and *termination* and that these in turn are broken down into *stages* specific to the industry or area of project application. In addition, the first two generic phases constitute project *planning,* while the last two constitute project realization or *accomplishment.* The nature of this project time frame and some of its special characteristics are discussed at greater length in PMBOK Handbook Volume 1, *A Framework for Project and Program Management Integration,* Chapters II and III.

The significance is that opportunity and risk generally remain relatively high during project planning but, because of the relatively low level of investment to this point, the amount at stake remains low. In contrast, during project accomplishment opportunity and risk progressively fall to lower levels as remaining unknowns are translated into knowns. At the same time, the amount at stake

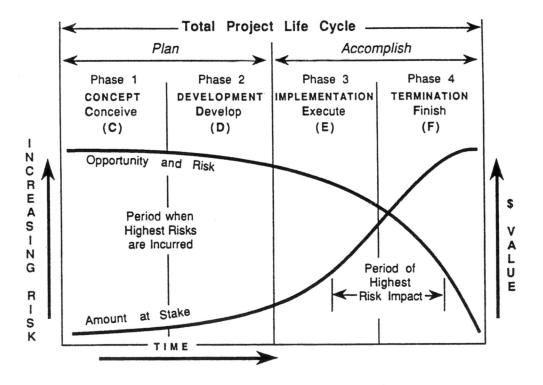

Figure II.2. Typical Life Cycle Profiles - Risk vs. Amount at Stake
R.M. Wideman, Project Management Course, 1990

steadily rises as the necessary resources are progressively invested to complete the project.

These trends are shown graphically in Figure II.2. The figure also shows that the period of highest vulnerability to risk occurs during the last two phases. At this time, adverse conditions may also be discovered as a result of acceptance testing and start-up of the project. The purpose of risk management must be to influence the project planning such that both uncertainty-risk and amount-at-stake are reduced to acceptable levels throughout the project life cycle.

F. Four-Phase Approach

In its most simplistic form, project risk management consists essentially of four process phases as shown in Figure II.3, namely:

- Identification
- Assessment
- Response, and
- Documentation

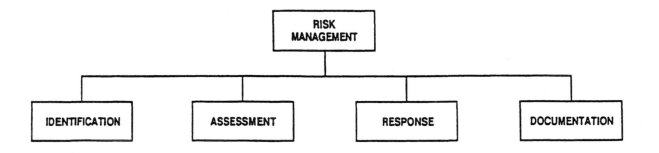

Figure II.3. Risk Function Breakdown: Four Processes

Phase One - Identification

This phase consists of identifying all the possible risks which may significantly impact the success of the project. Conceptually, these may range from high-impact/high-probability, through high-impact/low-probability, low-impact/high-probability to low-impact/low-probability. Obviously, the high and medium risks, including accumulations under any one item of risk, should receive the most attention. Moreover, combinations of risk which together pose a greater threat than each individually should not be overlooked.

In order to identify all the potential risks to a particular project, it may be necessary to undertake a risk identification program. This might involve soliciting the considered opinions of knowledgeable persons associated with the project or similar projects, or conducting a "brain-storming" type of workshop amongst the project team. But always remember, "the alligators that you do not see, are the ones that bite you!"

Phase Two - Assessment

Having identified the range of possible risks, the next step is to assess them. The purpose is to determine their ranking or status in terms of type, impact and probability. This may range from a simple attempt at subjective evaluation to a more serious attempt at measurement. Due to their nature, or simply through lack of relevant data, however, it may be found that many of the risks defy direct measurement and a more in-depth impact analysis becomes necessary.

Risk assessment typically involves input from all of project management functions, as shown in Figure II.1. Consequently, a major benefit of risk management, particularly early on in the project, is the integrating and team-building effect experienced by members of the project team.

Risk assessment methodology is discussed in Chapter IV and impact analysis is described in some detail in Appendix B. In addition, many sophisticated techniques have been developed in support of these processes, a number of which are briefly described in Appendix C.

Phase Three - Response

Mitigating project risk requires, first, establishing an appropriate system strategy, then taking out insurance as appropriate against those risks that are insurable, and finally, planning specific actions to deal with the remainder. These may range from simple decisions to accept the risks as they are, especially on a small project, to a comprehensive plan for deployment of resources to control a risk event, should it occur, where the event may be far reaching (e.g., labor strife) or urgent (e.g., fire, accident).

Phase Four - Documentation

Final documentation is a vital part of any project activity, though regretfully often overlooked. This is just as true of risk management. The purpose is to build a data base of reliable data for the continuing evaluation of risk on the current project, as well as for improving the data base for all subsequent projects.

Each of these phases are discussed in greater detail in the following chapters.

---

1. C. Quaife, text contributed September, 1989.
2. *PMBOK*, 3/28/87, p E-2.

Chapter III   Risk Identification

A. Risk in Corporate Business Management

In corporate business management, risk is typically divided into two basic types. The first of these, *Business Risk*, includes the inherent chances of both profit or loss associated with the particular business endeavor. Business entities employ staffs of specially trained managers, professionals, technicians, and skilled workers in order to increase the chances of profit and reduce the chances of loss. The essential purpose is to maximize profits.

The second type of risk is usually called *Pure*, or *Insurable Risk*. Insurable risk differs from business risk in that it involves only a chance for loss and no chance for profit. For example, insurable risks can be further divided into four general categories relating to the chances of loss: direct property, indirect property, liability, and personnel.

Obviously, direct property loss involves the destruction of property such as by fire, flood or wind storm. Indirect loss is somewhat more subtle and involves, for example, the extra expenses associated with renting alternative temporary accommodation or equipment following its damage or destruction, or the loss due to business interruption if operations cannot be continued because the replacement is not immediately available.

Liability loss, of course, involves the chance of a member of the public filing a lawsuit for bodily injury, personal injury, or property damage against the contractor. Finally, personal losses generally involve injuries to employees such as those contemplated by Worker's Compensation Laws.

B. Risk in Project Management

On most projects, responsibility for *Project Risk* is so pervasive that it is rarely given sufficient central attention. Moreover, the reader is reminded that not all risk events are independent. Indeed, the total amount at stake on a project may be highly dependent upon a series of interacting events. The old adage "It never rains but it pours!" is not an uncommon experience. In addition, a series of risk events can, and frequently do, cross traditional functional responsibility boundaries, which, with their classic difficulties of coordination and rapid response, can lead to disastrous consequences.

Ultimate responsibility for identifying risks to a project and their subsequent treatment must rest with the project sponsor. The very threat posed to the successful achievement of project objectives, as expressed in terms of scope, quality, time and cost, should be sufficient reason for the sponsor to recognize this responsibility.

A particular case of risk is where the project leader must take steps to keep the project on schedule, but must act with insufficient information to make a sound decision. Such risks should be calculated, not reckless, and the absence of the requisite information clearly recognized. It may be that the collection of the information is either too costly, too time consuming, or simply unavailable. In such situations it is advisable to have a contingency plan prepared so that when the information or results do become available, and they prove to be negative (i.e., bad news), there is a "fall-back" position to turn to.

In Research and Development projects, for example, unknowns that can turn into unpleasant surprises may include technical solutions that do not work as expected; experiments that fail; unanticipated by-products or side-effects, such as the undesirable side effects of a new drug; being eclipsed by an unanticipated superior product announcement, or by an overriding patent application by a competitor; market research indicating lack of customer acceptance; escalating product development costs; or simply product reliability, quality or producibility difficulties.

In R&D, some of these risks may be mitigated by conducting parallel development paths, with the view that if one approach does not work, then perhaps another will. This may cost more, but may be worth it in order to maintain flexibility, and so reduce the overall risk and elapsed development time.[1]

C. Types of Risk

Risks may be classified in a number of different ways. For example, one way is to describe uncertainties (and hence opportunities and risks) in terms of *knowns, known-unknowns,* and *unknown-unknowns*.

A known is an item or situation containing no uncertainty. An example of a known in our personal lives is death—it will happen and there is no uncertainty about it. Unknowns are those things which we know exist but do not know how they will affect us. A known-unknown is an identifiable uncertainty. An example of a known-unknown is our electricity bill—we know that we shall get one next month but do not how much it will be. Another example is cancer. We know that cancer exists, but do not know if we shall fall victim to it. An unknown-unknown is simply an item or situation whose existence we cannot imagine. For example, before the first case was reported, AIDS was an unknown-unknown. Now, however, since we know that AIDS exists, it is a known-unknown like cancer. Obviously, there can be no example of an unknown-unknown since, by definition, its existence cannot be imagined.[2]

The spectrum of risk events will obviously vary between projects, but projects are launched to take advantage of opportunities and, as explained earlier, opportunity and risk go together.

By their very nature projects are risky business. This interesting but simplistic approach is hardly adequate for project purposes, but it does underscore the fact that once all the risks seem to have been thought of there may still be a few remaining!

Another approach is to classify risks according to their impact on the project. For example:

- Scope risks – risks associated with changes of scope, or the subsequent need for "fixes" to achieve the required technical deliverables
- Quality risks – failure to complete tasks to the required level of technical or quality performance
- Schedule risks – failure to complete tasks within the estimated time limits, or risks associated with dependency network logic
- Cost risks – failure to complete tasks within the estimated budget allowances

Unfortunately, many identifiable risks will have an impact on two or more of these areas, particularly both schedule and cost, so that this leads to significant overlapping and potential double counting when it comes to making offsetting provisions.

Yet another way of classifying risks is to separate them according to their nature. For example, discrete one-time risk events such as fire and theft may be distinguished from those that are time-scaled, such as with flooding or earthquakes, because in the latter case the probability and magnitude of occurrence varies with the period of time selected. Such risks are typically insurable, and corporate management usually draws a distinction between insurable risk and business risk, where business risk is risk arising from the business venture itself.

Deliberately chosen risks, such as correctly identifying project objectives for a venture opportunity, may be distinguished from those which are latent, i.e., inherent in a situation or product, such as changes in market conditions or a faulty mechanical part.

Again, for any particular project, some risks may be considered to be sufficiently remote or catastrophic as to be outside of the realm of project responsibility. Obvious examples include a change in political direction or the financial collapse of the sponsoring organization.

D. Project Risk Identification

In order to deal systematically with the variety of risks encountered in project work, a more useful approach to risk identification is to classify the types of project risk according to primary source (rather than effect). This will also facilitate more effective management. The PMBOK categorizes sources of risk as follows:

- External, but unpredictable
- External predictable, but uncertain
- Internal - non-technical
- Technical
- Legal

It will be seen that this form of classification also provides the opportunity to rank the various risk groupings according to ability to manage effective response (i.e., their relative controllability). The degree of ability to manage the response is, of course, independent of probability, amount at stake and, hence, risk event status, discussed in Chapter II. This part of the risk management breakdown structure is shown in Figure III.1, with the groupings generally arranged from low ability to high. More detailed listings within these typical groupings are given in Appendix A.

The sequence of mitigation activities form the remainder of the risk management breakdown structure as shown in Figure III.2. These activities are discussed in subsequent chapters.

E. Project Risk Configuration

Identification of risks associated with a particular project commences with an understanding of the project itself. What is the project scope, i.e., the project deliverables, and indeed what are the underlying project objectives? Answers to these questions will have significant impact on the selection of probable risks to be considered on the project, and, in particular, will impact decisions on alternative project strategies and work-arounds for identified problems.

For example, in selecting a system for project delivery, e.g., in-house resources or outside single or multiple contracts, is the underlying objective to:

- Maximize return on investment, as in a commercial venture to supply goods;
- Minimize cost and financial risk, as in the case of a project undertaken by a non-profit organization;

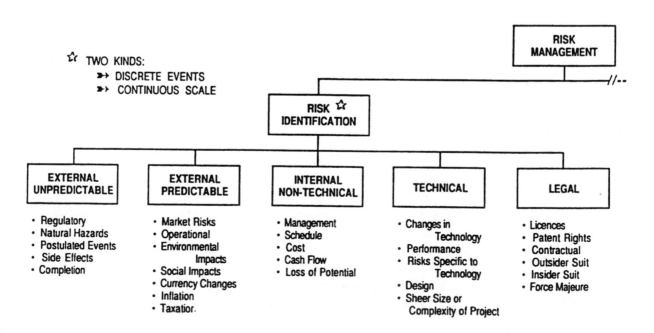

Figure III.1. Risk Management Identification

- Maximize reliability with minimum production downtime, as with a public utility;
- Maximize safety with minimum environmental impact, as with a public transportation service; or
- Maximize flexibility and use of internal resources, as in the case of a commercial service to the public?

Such questions must be established at a very early stage of the project, and the answers and resulting decisions themselves often must be made in a high degree of uncertainty requiring qualitative judgement. In any case, the results will have a considerable effect on the risk characteristics of the project. These decisions, properly handled, typically involve multidisciplinary effort, and perhaps specialists who are required to examine the project in detail.

In a significant and beneficial integrative risk management effort, information flows from one group to another in the form of most-likely estimates of project parameters. Gradually, an overall approach is built up around these estimates, which may then be tested against other possible criteria, such as sensitivity to economic conditions, including prices and demand; competition; life cycle economics; other project alternatives; and so on.

The technical configuration of the project may also be subject to design alternatives, in which appropriate questions would be:

- With respect to which project parameters is this design feature required?
- What is the likelihood of variation of the referenced parameters, and hence the need of the design feature as described?

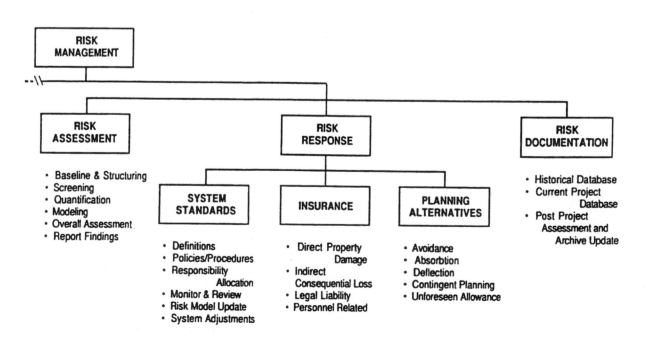

Figure III.2. Risk Management: Mitigation

- What is the likelihood that this design feature will perform as expected?
- What are the implications of this feature on project parameters and objectives which constitute project success?

From these questions, the costs, benefits and risks of a particular design feature can be evaluated under various scenarios and the relative benefit determined.

None of these questions can be answered properly, however, unless they have been dealt with early in the project planning and evaluation phase, and explicit estimates made of the implications.

F. Risk Factors

All project risks are characterized by the following three *risk factors:*[3]

1. *Risk event* – precisely what might happen to the detriment of the project;
2. *Risk probability* – how likely the event is to occur; and
3. *Amount at stake* – the severity of the consequences.

With this data, the *risk event status* (criterion value or ranking) of a given risk event can be determined by the following relationship:

Risk Event Status = Risk Probability x Amount at Stake

Some risk events are characterized by low probability and high severity, while others are the reverse. Clearly, the most serious risks are those involving both high probability and high severity. As noted earlier, many risk events cannot be treated as simply discrete and independent as the total amount at stake may increase substantially as a result of a series of interacting events. Such a situation calls for careful examination and special analytical techniques.

---

1. W.N. Hosley, All-Tech Project Management Services, in letter dated April 19, 1990.
2. M.W. Curran, Decision Sciences Corporation, in letter dated November 26, 1990.
3. D.C. Fraser, Risk Minimisation in Giant Projects, International Conference on the Successful Accomplishment of Giant Projects, London, England, May 1978.

Chapter IV   Risk Assessment Goals and Methodology

A. Risk Assessment Goals

The goals of risk assessment are to:

- Increase the understanding of the project in general.
- Identify the alternatives available in delivery and methods.
- Ensure that uncertainties and risks are adequately considered in a structured and systematic way, which allows them to be incorporated into the planning and project development process.
- Through direct examination of these uncertainties and risks, establish the implications of these on all other aspects of the project.

Major benefits of these goals include:

- Greater information is made available during the course of project planning and decision making; for example, estimates of uncertainty of project performance and viability should evolve;
- The project objectives themselves may be called into question, and hence improved upon;
- Improved communication between members of the project team, and other project stakeholders, where appropriate;
- Confidence that the true implications of uncertainties and risk have been examined and incorporated into the project plans;
- Documented support for the project contingency allowance, and a basis for its application management;
- Reduced probability that the realization of the project will be sub-optimal, either by identifying weaknesses or by forcing improvements during the project planning phases;
- Consequently, a reduced likelihood of disruptive changes during implementation;
- Hence, substantially increased chances of project success.

Properly handled, the risk assessment process should promote the language of probability and the use of its associated mathematics in risk analysis. It is best handled by examining the individual elements of the project in some detail and determining their relationships, because most people are more able to comprehend the parts than the whole. In a formal quantitative risk assessment, i.e., a risk impact analysis, a mathematical means is developed to integrate the complex relationships between the detailed elements of available information and the information possessed by numerous experts while preserving the experts' uncertainty of opinion.[1]

Bear in mind that the objective of project management is always to achieve project success through "participant satisfaction." Since the long-term viability of the resulting product is often a key element of success, it may also be necessary to conduct a comprehensive product life cycle risk analysis during the conceptual phase of the project. This would be particularly true if the project is large and/or complex, the product has an extended life as in building and engineering works, or is part of an extended program of projects. In this case the project risk assessment, which essentially covers the functions of technical scope, quality, time and cost, may form part of this more comprehensive product risk analysis.

B. Assessment Methodology

Selection

Perhaps the greatest impediment to the acceptance of risk management as a normal part of project management is the realization that project risks are so many and various that more than superficial traditional attention might thwart the project at the outset. This attitude denies the contribution that closer examination of some of the risks to a particular project can bestow on its ultimate success. The issue is: Having identified possibly a large number of risks, which should receive attention?

In fact, no risks should be entirely ignored, but many of the lesser risks can be provided for by the conventional contingency allowance approach. Clearly, the risks that should receive the closest attention are those that could have both the greatest impact on the project as well as the most likely probability of occurrence. To some extent, the selection of these particular risks is an iterative process in which preliminary analysis may indicate the need for further study. Figure IV.1 shows a conceptual flow diagram in which risk events are first categorized and then assessed for severity and probability in order to arrive at a criterion value on which a priority ranking can be based.

The extent of the assessment at this stage should be governed by the project's risk management policies, but in any case, the categorization should be closely aligned to the project's work breakdown structure. Consequently, the possibility of a significant impact as a result of some combination of apparently minor events must not be overlooked. For example, a succession of relatively insignificant schedule delays, perhaps as a consequence of a spate of untimely scope changes, could become highly significant. The effect could be to completely miss a "window of opportunity" such as reaching a market before a competitor, forestalling technological obsolescence, or construction in the summer season rather than in winter.

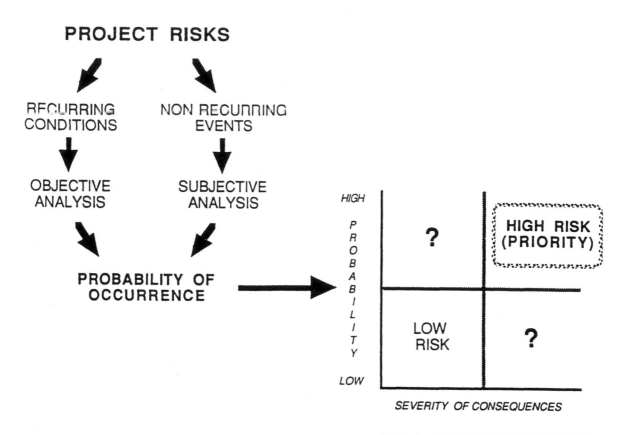

Figure IV.1. Comparing Severity of Project Risks

R.M. Wideman, Project Management Course, 1991

Simple Assessment Development

A simple risk assessment may be conducted by stepping through the sequence shown in Figure IV.2. As a prelude to a better understanding of the relative significance of the findings, however, a Risk Baseline should be established based on the organization's external "status quo." This will establish the risks to the sponsoring organization associated with not carrying out the project at all. The internal intrinsic worth of the project should also be documented.

Step 1

Select the risk events, or series of related events, to be examined. Prioritize these for attention according to the initial selection discussed earlier.

Certain risk events may be screened out from further consideration, as a matter of policy, even though the event could have a major impact. For example, an "out-of-scope" risk event might be one that seriously impacts other activities of the sponsoring organization, or is common to more than one project. In this case appropriate response planning might be incorporated into the organization's business planning, rather than at the project level, to avoid overlap and duplication. Blanket corporate insurance coverage is a prime example.

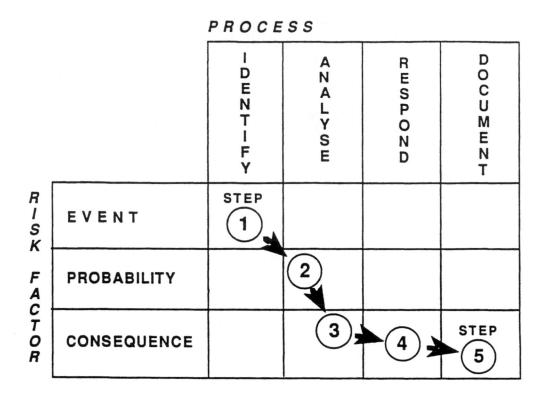

Figure IV.2. Impact Analysis Matrix Sequence

Step 2

Assess the probability associated with the risk event(s). This is perhaps one of the more subjective steps, although there are a number of procedures which can help. An estimate of the degree of uncertainty may be arrived at by:

- Influence diagrams
- Risk contribution analysis
- Probability distribution
- Probability trees
- Risk modelling
- Sensitivity profiles

Where the determination of probability is particularly elusive, but important, there are more elaborate techniques available as described in Appendix C. Beware, however, of overconfidence in the accuracy of the results of these various approaches. At best, they are estimates based on good experience and thoughtful opinion.

Step 3

Assess the consequences and severity of the risk event(s) by determining:

- the amount at stake, and
- the criticality.

Note that amount at stake and criticality may vary with time, i.e., according to the stage in the project life cycle, as discussed earlier in Chapter II.E.

In most cases, the amount at stake and criticality can be arrived at by a simple examination of the available data and some subjective judgment. In complex situations, however, it may be necessary to develop some form of mathematical model and conduct a series of computer runs.

Step 4

Having identified the consequences and their significance, this step involves planning to mitigate the likelihood of the risk event(s) in question, and/or developing suitable responses and contingency plans, as discussed in Chapter VI. It may even be necessary to gain more insight and gather additional information to complete this step. Either way, it should be the most creative step of all because it provides the occasion for converting risks into opportunities.

Step 5

The final step in the process is to accumulate the results of the assessment in a set of "Conclusions and Recommendations" such that appropriate management decisions can be made with full knowledge of the apparent risks involved. Either the residual risks must be accepted, or the project abandoned.

By following these steps the management of risk and uncertainty can be directly incorporated into the early project planning process as well as dealt with expeditiously during the course of project execution.

Risk Quantification

The application of the various techniques noted in Steps 2 and 3 above can provide insight into risk event interdependencies, the merits of further detailed consideration of specific risks, and the manner in which combined effects of risk events might be modelled mathematically. In such an analysis, especially on large projects, it is often necessary to develop a further breakdown in which each activity is numbered and documented for reference. Using this breakdown, the risks within each activity are identified by mentally stepping through all aspects of the activity to produce a comprehensive list of uncertainties.

As with the project work breakdown structure, this breakdown serves to focus discussion, to aid in identification of all risks, and to provide a basis for formalizing dependency links within the project. In this way a model may be developed in which the variables are represented by discrete probability distributions having specified linkages. This allows maximum flexibility in representing distribution shapes as well as offering mathematical simplicity. It also paves the way for solving complex combinations of dependent and independent variables by repetitive computerized calculations.

Where risk combination is analyzed by such modelling, three levels of model are typically required. These are:

1. For detailed analysis of the joint impact of a small number of risks within an activity,
2. For examining the joint effects of all risks within an activity, and
3. For examining the broad overall impact of risks from several or all activities.

This can be conceptualized as the successive summarization of a large probability tree and the resulting output shows overall distributions as they impact cost, schedule and quality. These distributions can be displayed graphically so as to show the relative importance of each contributing risk, as well as their cumulative effect. Such risk analysis is discussed in more detail in Appendix B.

In-depth project risk impact analyses are generally the purview of specialists in risk analysis who are familiar with the various technical aspects of the project management application in question. This may require a significant commitment of time and resources and may only be appropriate where there is substantial uncertainty, the stakes are high, and there is a need for significant management attention.

C. Advantages of Assessment Methodology

From the foregoing it can be seen that there are additional benefits which derive from this assessment methodology by providing:

1. The vehicle for incorporating uncertainties directly into the project management process of planning, development and implementation of the project
2. A clear understanding of the overall project's goals, objectives, scope definition and feasibility
3. What the risks really are, which are the most significant, and hence which should receive attention to lead to the most risk reduction
4. The models and techniques by which the variability and uncertainty of estimates can be conveyed quantitatively
5. An information base of quantitative and order-of-magnitude data to support trade-off decisions, such as choices between cost and performance, or the comparison of different options
6. A more rational basis for contingency planning and evaluation
7. A more consistent and workable project plan
8. An early warning for risk

It is better to avoid risks now than to encounter them later.

D. The Basics of Probability

Probability may apply to simple on/off or go/no-go type situations such as getting approval or not getting approval, or it may be more complex and apply to ranges of probability as encountered in estimating time and cost.[2]

Simple Probability

To provide a better understanding of simple probability, consider the following question and answer: "What is the probability that we shall get approval for our project next month?" "It looks good, say, about 75%!" So what is the estimated probability of this event occurring? 75%? However, it also means that there is a 25% probability that approval will not be obtained. Note that the probability of the event occurring Pr(Event) plus the probability of the event not happening Pr(No Event) equals one—always.

What if there are two related events? For example, consider the following question and answer: "What is the probability that we shall have the scope defined by next month and that we shall get approval?" "Well, it still looks pretty good, say, about 80% that it will be ready and 70% that we shall get approval." If the two events are possible but not certain, then how likely is it that they will both happen?

$$Pr(Event\ \#1) \times Pr(Event\ \#2) = Pr(Both\ Events)$$

But Pr(Event #1) is 80%, and Pr(Event #2) is 70%, so how likely is it that both will happen?

$$0.70 \times 0.80 = 0.56 = 56\%.$$

That's barely over a 50-50 chance. Suppose that only one of these things is necessary before starting project planning. What is the probability that we shall start project planning?

$$Pr(No\ Scope) \times Pr(No\ Approval) = Pr(No\ Planning)$$
$$0.30 \quad \times \quad 0.20 \quad = \quad 0.06 \quad = 6\%$$

The probability that neither will happen is very low, so it is 94% likely that we will start planning.

Another way to look at this problem is in three parts:

$$
\begin{array}{llll}
Pr(Scope) & \times\ Pr(Approval) & = 0.70 \times 0.80 & = 0.56 \\
Pr(Scope) & \times\ Pr(No\ Approval) & = 0.70 \times 0.20 & = 0.14 \\
Pr(No\ Scope) & \times\ Pr(Approval) & = 0.30 \times 0.80 & = \underline{0.24} \\
& & & 0.94 \\
& & & or\ \ 94\%\ likely
\end{array}
$$

More Complex Probability

Probability ranges are more complex to deal with, especially in project work. For example, if a given human activity is repeated many times, ostensibly under identical conditions, then the actual durations experienced will nevertheless not be identical. This variation will be due to a number of influences impacting the activity such as human productivity. Theoretically, if the frequency of occurrence (i.e., the number of times that a particular duration occurs) is plotted against the time taken for the activity, the resulting plot will produce a "Gaussian" distribution curve, popularly known as a *bell curve*. The bell curve is typically symmetrical about its highest frequency value, in which case it is described as a *normal* distribution.

The probability of any particular time being taken is, strictly speaking, its number of occurrences divided by the total number of times the activity was repeated in the whole sample. This fraction may be expressed as a percentage. For example, the probability (chances) of landing a "heads" or "tails" in a coin toss is 0.5 or 50%. Similarly, the chances of pulling any given playing card from a full deck is 1 in 52, or approximately 2%.

In project work, two practical difficulties arise with the application of this theory. In the first place, a set of observations rarely exists upon which a discrete probability calculation can be made, and rarely is there the opportunity to carry out repeated runs of an activity during project planning in order to make the calculation. Consequently, where future events are being postulated, it is necessary to rely on speculation.

This leads to the second difficulty. When people are asked to speculate on probability, there is typically a tendency to be optimistic. This may be due to natural human optimism, but is more likely due to it being easier to overlook obstacles than it is to account for them. Consequently, such bell curves of probability are rarely symmetrical. Two examples are shown in Figure V.1, Chapter V. These probability distribution curves show the many values that an element might take. The concept is used in Range Estimating (see Chapter V.C).

When speculating on the probability of future events, it is usual to establish three values in order to fix the shape of the curve. These values are the two outer limits of the element plus the value which has the highest probability of occurrence, i.e. the "most likely." This simpler approach is used in PERT calculations (see Chapter V.B).

Two examples of how these might be expressed:

• The cost of project planning will fall between $x and $y with the cost distributed "normally" around $z;
• Activity #B116 has a low value of "o" days, a high value of "p" days, a most likely value of "m" days with a triangular (square, stepped, bell, etc.) distribution.

The "mean" of a probability distribution curve (i.e., the value at which there is 50% of the total area under the curve on each side) is known as its "expected value," and this expected value is found by taking:

(the value an element can take) x
                    (probability that it will take that value)

then summing the results, i.e., the expected value is the "weighted average" (possible values weighted by their likelihood of occurrence).

The "most likely" value referred to earlier is that value which has the most likelihood of occurring. It is only the same as the "expected value" if the distribution is symmetrical around the "most likely."

Note that the sum of the "means" (expected values) is the mean of the sums (total). That is, if the total cost of a project = the sum of WBS items #1-100, then the "expected" total cost is the same as the sum of the "expected" costs for each WBS item #1-100 since these are all arrived at by calculation from the given observations. The sum of the separate "most likely" values, on the other hand, is not necessarily the "most likely" for the whole project.

When all is said and done, the project manager should be wary of false impressions of accuracy generated by extensive calculations. The assessment of the probability of an event occurring is only as good as the available historic data upon which the assessment is based, or the quality of the experience and opinions of those making the assessment.

E. The Quality Risk

The goals of risk management are to increase understanding of the project, hence improve project plans, system delivery selection, and especially to identify where the greatest risks are likely to occur during the phases of project accomplishment. This helps to establish where management can best focus its attention during the project and much of that attention will be concentrated on containing potential overruns of schedule and cost. Presuming that the project is not complete until the entire scope is accomplished, there will nevertheless still remain a major area of project risk.

This risk can best be expressed by the question: "What if the project fails to perform as expected during its operational life?" This may well be the result of less than satisfactory quality upon project completion, and is especially true if quality is not given due attention during the project life cycle. Since the in-service life of the resulting product is typically much longer than the period required to plan and produce that product, any quality shortcomings and their effects may surface over a prolonged period of time.

Consequently, of all the project objectives, conformance to quality requirements is the one most remembered long after cost and schedule performance have faded into the past. It follows that quality management can have the most impact on the long-term actual or perceived success of the project.

This may be demonstrated by considering the long-term cash flow, including project costs, of a commercial venture as displayed in Figure IV.3. As the figure shows, the intended return-on-investment could be thwarted by "poor" quality. Quality risk impacts may remain hidden or ignored, but are not forgiven if the project fails to deliver its long-term objectives.

F. The Schedule Risk

It is possible to manage the "critical path" of a schedule activity network but not manage the project duration. This is

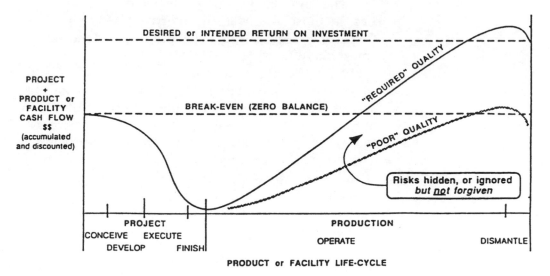

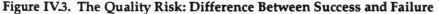

Figure IV.3. The Quality Risk: Difference Between Success and Failure

because the schedule risk[3] is the "highest risk path" that contributes the most risk to project completion, and this path is not necessarily the critical path as determined by simple network analysis. In fact, the "likelihood of finishing on time" requires examination of the risks associated with all the activities necessary to reach completion.

There is risk in the duration of every activity because any duration in the future is uncertain. Therefore, duration must be measured as a range, and this is typically expressed in terms of the low, most likely (or alternatively, expected) and high durations associated with specified degrees of certainty. The extent to which the high-risk durations impact project completion will depend on the logical relationships between activities and the skillful management of available float.

Note that the longest activities are not necessarily the "riskiest" (a long-duration activity could be quite reliable). Indeed, any activity may be "highly risky," and any such activity could delay the project, whether or not it is on the critical path. Therefore, it is necessary to identify and manage all the activities that could contribute to the most delay to the project, which are not necessarily those on the critical path as observed earlier. This suggests that where significant project activity risks are involved a standard "critical path method" (CPM) may be of only limited value. However, the CPM approach could suffice if the "expected" (calculated) durations are used rather than the "most likely" (see Section D above for discussion of "expected" and "most likely").

After considering significant activity duration risks on a particular project, it is quite possible that a sound management strategy would be to forego the "expected" completion date by several days in order to reduce the overall project risk. To make this determination it would be necessary to combine activity risks along alternative paths of the schedule network. On simple networks this is relatively easy but for complex networks the process is not self-evident nor intuitive.

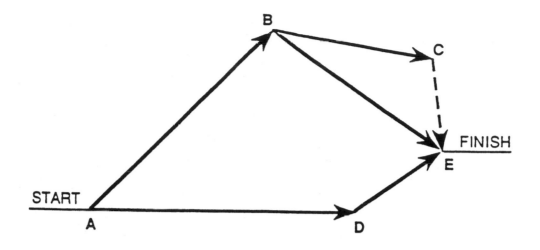

Figure IV.4. Simple Example of Network Completion Risk
(MacKrimmon and Ryavec in Archibald & Villoria)
D.T. Hulett, PMP Certification Workshop - Risk Management, PMI Orange County Chapter, 1991, p52.

Consider the activity network shown in Figure IV.4, having low, most likely and high durations as shown in Table IV.1, Network Activity Summary. Calculated means assuming a symmetrical distribution are shown in the fifth column of the table.

Table IV.1. Network Activity Summary

ACTIVITY	LOW	MOST LIKELY	HIGH	MEAN EXPECTED
A-B	8	9	10	9
B-C	4	5	6	5
C-E	0	0	0	0
B-E	1	6	7	4.7
A-D	4	9	14	9
D-E	1	2	7	3.3

Three ways of evaluating duration along alternative network paths are shown in Table IV.2, Network Path Evaluation. The question is, which path is the most risky? The exercise gives multiple answers and, hence, mixed signals.

Table IV.2. Network Path Evaluation

PATH	SUM OF MOST LIKELY	SUM OF MEANS	SUM OF HIGHS
A-B-C-E	14	14	16
A-B-E	15	13.7	17
A-D-E	11	12.3	21
MOST RISKY	A-B-E	A-B-C-E	A-D-E

The example is used simply to demonstrate that in the face of considerable uncertainty more sophisticated calculations are needed in which degrees of uncertainty can be specified, probability distributions assigned, and relative activity risks assessed. Computerized mathematical models can be constructed to deal with these variables, but software is also now available off-the-shelf to assist the project manager by creating a number of probability projections expressed as "S" curves (see Handbook Volume 1, Chapter VII.F). The collective result to any given degree of certainty is then represented by the envelope of overriding values, i.e., those generated by the riskiest near-critical activities.

1. After D.T. Hulett, PMP Certification Workshop - Risk Management, PMI Orange County
       Chapter, 1991, p19.
2. Ibid., p3.
3. Ibid., p46-53.

Chapter V   Computer Applications

A. Data Storage, Retrieval and Computation

The use of computers, and microcomputers in particular, has gained ground rapidly in recent years due to the very rapid increase in the power of micro hardware. This has stimulated the development of elegant software capable of storing data in flat readily-accessible data bases, or rapidly executing complex calculations which can produce robust graphical output. All of this greatly facilitates communication, an essential ingredient of successful project management.

The capacity of the computer simply to store information for subsequent retrieval is invaluable. Most projects involve large amounts of data which once associated with it become unique to that project. If data can be collected and subsequently readily searched and distributed to meet the progressive information requirements on the evolving project, this in itself can go a long way towards avoiding the risks of mistakes, misunderstandings and misdirections. Data of this sort typically includes agreements, instructions, specifications, drawings, latest changes, progress coordination, current priorities, and so on.

Powerful and sophisticated software is now available on the desk-top to support complex scheduling, range estimating and costing, spread sheet type calculations, statistical quality analysis and, more recently, the possibility of artificial intelligence applications (see Chapter X.C).

The computer helps members of the project team to reduce the drudgery and time involved in handling large amounts of data and wearisome calculations. It also helps rapid retrieval of vital information for decision making. In addition, personal computers are establishing an increasing role in the transfer of electronic data and, together with the related "fax" machine, in the speed and reliability of project communications.

B. PERT and the Probabilistic Model

One of the earlier applications of the computer was to the PERT schedule network analysis technique. PERT stands for Program and Evaluation Review Technique, a technique which was originally developed for complex projects with an innovative content and a high degree of uncertainty. Today, the term PERT Chart tends to be misapplied in some software descriptions to refer to a project schedule when presented in the form of a logic network. This is to distinguish it from a Gantt Chart, which presents the same data but in the form of a bar chart, i.e., horizontal bars representing activities plotted against time.

The real significance of the PERT technique is that it recognizes that estimates of activity time durations are just that—estimates. As was shown in Chapter I.C, opportunity and risk are closely allied and in a probabilistic world a "most likely" estimate has by definition an equal value set of opportunities and risks that define the "best case" and "worst case." Some risks will inevitably come true as will some opportunities so, as noted earlier, project management must constantly pursue the latter to offset the former.[1]

This concept is reflected in the PERT technique by establishing for each activity in the network three time estimates which represent:

- The most optimistic time possible for the activity, o,
- Its most likely time, m, and
- The most pessimistic time, p.

If these three estimates are represented by time durations of o, m, and p, respectively, PERT allocates four times the weight to the most likely so that the expected time is then given by:

$$Expected\ Time = \frac{o + 4m + p}{6}$$

A more complete discussion describing the application of the PERT methodology to cost and schedule analysis, with simple worked examples, is provided in Appendix D. Yet, this technique gives rise to a fair amount of calculation, even for a relatively small network, so it is ideally suited to the computer. However, just calculating the uncertainties of activity durations (and costs) may not be sufficient. The consequences need to be worked through the project network logic. There are a number of software packages on the market that use network simulation using probabilistic evaluation of success-dependent logic to arrive at possible results, or to evaluate various alternative "what if" scenarios involving uncertainties. Such tools help to give insight into the sensitivities of the variables for purposes of project planning.

C. Range Estimating

The application of probabilistic modeling to cost estimates is employed in the Range Estimating approach,[2] which is used as an adjunct to traditional estimating and not a substitute for it. The methodology relies heavily upon the application of Pareto's Law, Monte Carlo simulation and heuristics to identify:

- The mathematical probability that a cost overrun will occur
- The amount of financial exposure (how bad it can get)
- Risks and opportunities ranked in order of bottom line importance
- The contingency required for a given level of confidence

An assessment is first made of the maximum tolerable variation in an estimate's bottom-line total cost which might result from a variation in any single element of that estimate. This threshold value is called the critical variance. The critical elements in the estimate are then identified as those whose actual values could vary from the target by such a magnitude that the bottom-line cost of the project would change by an amount greater than the critical variance. At a given level of probability, the variations in the actual values will be either favorable or unfavorable and will range from highest to lowest.

The deciding factor is not necessarily the magnitude of the element itself but its potential for variation. Consequently, the number of such elements in a typical estimate is not very large. Nevertheless, because of the large number of possible combinations, the number of potential outcomes in the actual bottom-line cost is indeed very large. Using a computer, these individual uncertainties are put together in such a way that the uncertainty in the bottom-line total can be measured.

The range of the resulting estimate is a simple but effective measure of its uncertainty. Surprisingly, the entire process requires only a modest amount of effort. Figure V.1 shows the probability distributions of two projects both of which have the same 50 percent probability of being completed for the expected value of $165,000. However, because of their respective distributions, project A is more likely to be completed close to the expected value than project B because the latter is less certain. Project B will require a higher contingency amount to achieve the same level of confidence in the estimate as project A.

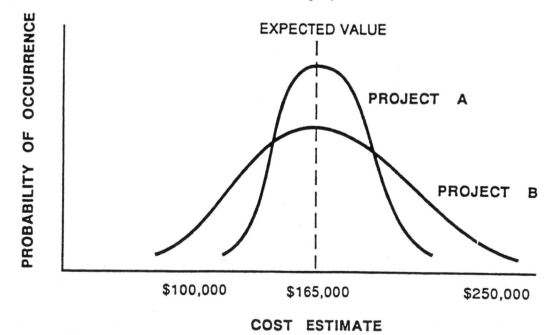

Figure V.1. Probability Distributions: Two Projects With the Same Expected Values of Total Costs
After J.R. Adams and M.D. Martin, A Practical Approach to the Assessment of Project Uncertainty, PMI Seminar/Symposium, Toronto, 1982, pIV-F.6

D. Risk Analysis

Risk analysis, especially as described in Appendix B, is particularly suited to computerization because it permits large amounts of data to be both stored and manipulated. Data is usually entered interactively in response to question/prompts at each stage, and such that it can be rapidly changed to suit different requirements, or "what if" enquiries. The computer also provides the automatic ability to present the results graphically, instead of through seemingly endless streams of hard-to-comprehend printouts.

Data to be handled might include:

- Different project configurations
- Different damage/response scenarios and consequences for each configuration
- Associated risk probabilities
- Data for translation to equivalent dollar costs or time
- Calculations of probability distributions, either in terms of some natural value (e.g., lost time or materials), project dollar costs, or project schedule delay.

Since the amount of data produced by these calculations is typically enormous, a variety of plotted output formats greatly simplifies presentation. For example, in Figure B.1 (Appendix B) a set of histograms shows the probability level identified for each risk event magnitude. Figure B.2 shows the probability of damage level if the risk event occurs, and Figure B.3 shows the probability of the criterion value being realized if the particular damage level is realized. For the case illustrated, calculating the effects of a single risk in each of, say, five configurations, at five risk levels,

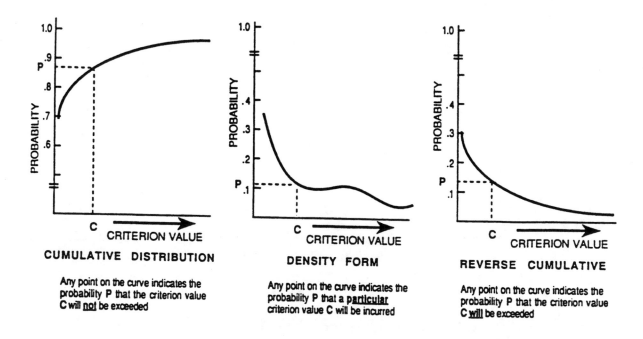

Figure V.2. Graphical Presentation of Analysis Results

After A.B. Cammaert c. 1986

and five damage scenarios, at three criterion levels, would involve 375 calculations for the one type of risk alone. Figure V.1. shows alternative formats for presenting such probability analysis results graphically. Figure V.2 illustrates cumulative risks plotted by source category to show how the criterion values vary with degree of certainty.

E. Knowledge-Based Risk Management

In our post-industrial information-intensive age, corporate planning and decision making appear to be dominated by high-powered information technology based on worldwide database retrieval networks and powerful computers. Through such networks and databases, almost all required data can readily be obtained, except, that is, knowledge that domain specialists have obtained through experience. Recently, *artificial intelligence* (AI), or its sub-specialty, *expert systems* (also called knowledge-based systems) has attracted special interest in order to deal with such domain specialists' knowledge.

The expert system provides an integrated approach which facilitates risk identification by generating a list of the most significant uncertainty factors and their descriptions. This list includes the principal risks of all major parties involved in a project, including the uncertainty factors that affect productivity, cost, schedule, quality, and performance. The user selects factors related

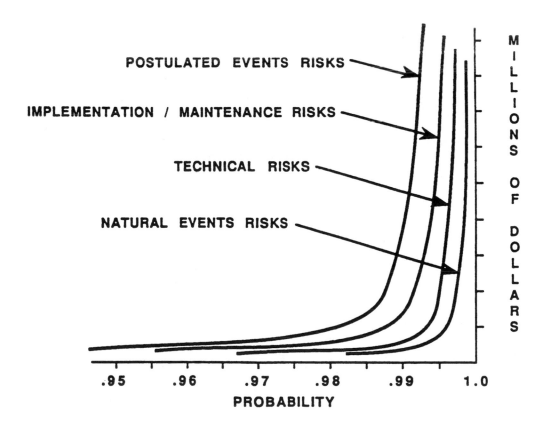

Figure V.3. Presenting Results of Analysis: Cumulative Risks vs. Criterion Value - Construction Project

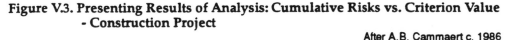

After A.B. Cammaert c. 1986

to a given project from the list. Each of the general factors is further divided into subelements which provide the user with added detail. After identifying the uncertainty factors, the expert system goes on to ask questions about risk policy, and so on.[3]

Figure V.4. shows an example of the breakdown structure of an expert system inference net for construction risk management.

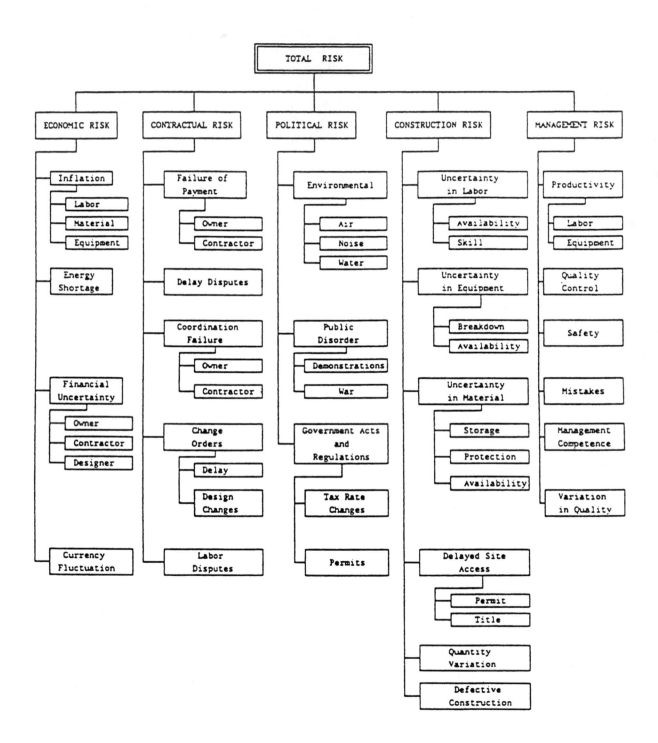

Figure V.4. Breakdown Structure of Identified Risks
After R. Kangari and L.T. Boyer, Risk Management by Expert Systems,
PMJ, March 1989, p41

Application of expert systems in risk management can provide a practical model which not only considers traditional models, but also expert knowledge, rules of thumb, and professional experiences. An expert system provides information which is necessary for management to make decisions under the condition of uncertainty.

In his book, *Knowledge-Based Risk Management*,[4] Kiyoshi Niwa develops the concept of a common expert system, then identifies the weak points in terms of ill-structured management domains. He then proposes a new concept of *human-computer cooperative system* to overcome these weak points. The key element is incorporating human intuitive ability into a computer system to improve its flexibility and applicability. Specifically, the system includes:

- A knowledge base
- A computer inference function
- Human intuitive ability
- A human-computer cooperative system to associate computer-generated inference and non-logical human intuition

The purpose of the system is to facilitate the calculation of risks and improved management responses in the execution of projects by commanding more comprehensive data.

1. P. Buckley, in a written response to the first draft of this handbook.
2. M.W. Curran, Range Estimating: Measuring Uncertainty and Reasoning with Risk, *Cost Engineering*, Vol. 31, No. 3, March 1989, p18-26, and in a letter dated November 26, 1990.
3. R. Kangari and L.T. Boyer, Risk Management by Expert Systems, *PMJ*, March 1989, p40-48.
4. K. Niwa, *Knowledge-Based Risk Management in Engineering*, John Wiley & Sons, New York, 1989, p ix.

Chapter VI   Risk Response and Documentation

A. Response Options

The structure of project risk response was shown diagrammatically in Figure III.2, Chapter III. Conceptually, responses to project risks identified and evaluated as a result of the steps described in previous chapters may take any of the following forms. A risk may be:

- Unrecognized, unmanaged or ignored (by default)
- Recognized but no action taken (absorbed as a matter of policy)
- Avoided (by taking appropriate steps)
- Reduced (by an alternative approach)
- Shared (with others, e.g., by joint venture)
- Transferred (to others through contract or insurance)
- Retained and absorbed (by prudent allowances)
- Handled by a combination of the above

Certainly the choice will depend on the project, the risks and the circumstances, but the selection should be based on a clearly defined set of standards.

B. System Standards

The next step, then, is to set policies, procedures, goals and responsibility standards for risk management on the project in question. Where appropriate, risk policy should be based on the principle that responsibility should be placed on the shoulders of those who represent the source of the risk in question. This will establish the scope and framework for the risk management function, whether it is simply a recognition of a task to be undertaken by the project manager, or the responsibility of a specialist or team under his direction.

Bear in mind that risk events will affect the project's cost, schedule, or quality of the work to an extent which depends on the event and how it is handled. The overall project risk will also vary considerably through the project life cycle, as described in Chapter II.E. Potential impacts will increase as tasks with risk events of high probability are undertaken and then decrease as the bulk of the work is completed.

The project risk may also change substantially as a result of changes in the scope of the project or changes in the method of working. Consequently, continuous review of the situation, with appropriate adjustments, is strongly recommended.

Generally speaking, project risk policies and procedures should encourage the following preferred actions as appropriate:

- Develop an environment and/or work-arounds designed to avoid or minimize selected risk events
- Reduce impacts by defensive planning
- Transfer the effect to others having control over the risk source
- Make appropriate allowance for retained residual risks
- Provide some flexibility in the contingency allowance procedures to permit some response to the unexpected

The term *work-around* may need some explanation. A work-around is an alternative solution to a potential problem—"We can get around that by doing this." For example, Requirements: Provide airtight food container. Solution: Sheet metal box with tight-fitting lid. Risk: Nonavailability. *Work-around: Substitute durable molded plastic container with self-sealing top.*

C. Insurance

Those types of risk which are insurable can be selected from the list of possible risks to the project, and duly insured. For example:[1]

1. Direct Property Damage
   - resulting from auto collision
   - or other auto events
   - to equipment, in transit or handling, etc.
   - to project materials, including theft
   - to contractors' property

2. Indirect Consequential Loss
   - cost of removing direct loss debris
   - equipment replacement
   - rental income loss
   - business interruption
   - liquidated damages
   - increased financing

3. Legal Liability
   - public bodily harm
   - property damage arising from the negligence of others
   - personal injury arising from the negligence of others
   - damage to the project entity due to
   - design errors
   - execution errors
   - project failure to perform as specified

4. Personnel-Related
   - employee bodily injury
   - cost to replace employee
   - resulting business loss

D. Response Planning

As a result of the methodology outlined above, a picture of project risk will emerge. This will include where, when, and to what extent exposure may be anticipated.

With this picture in hand it is then possible to formulate suitable risk management strategies, whether by way of absorption, adjustment, deflection or systematic contingency planning. Adjustment may simply involve the proper recognition of certain risks by appropriate modifications to the project's scope, budget, schedule, and quality specification, or all four combined.

Adequate contingency allowance and good control, even on a tight budget, will reduce the chance of overrun. A logically developed schedule with attention to resource requirements and conflicts will reduce the probability of schedule overrun. But in the course of the enthusiastic initiation of project implementation, how often has one heard the battle cry "Our objective is to build the best there is!" Not surprisingly, such an unrealistic definition of quality results in a very high risk indeed of the project being unsuccessful due to cost and time overruns as well as possible failure to achieve even more realistic performance objectives!

Deflection involves the transfer of risk by such means as:

- Contracting out to another party
- Insurance or bonding, or
- By recognizing it in the contract

In the latter case, caution is advised since experience shows that this strategy will only be cost-effective if the contractor has proper and effective control over the source of the risk or risks concerned.

Contingent planning includes:

- The management of a contingency budget
- The development of schedule alternatives and work-arounds
- Complete emergency responses to deal with major specific areas of risk
- An assessment of project shut-down liabilities

In complex situations, the effects of all such strategies can, if required, be analyzed by making appropriate changes to the risk model suggested in Chapter IVB.3. In this way decisions can be optimized and the project can proceed with increased confidence.

E. Data Collection, Application and Documentation

1. Historical Databases

Project risk management, particularly the risk evaluation and analysis activities, is data intensive. A reliable data source or sources is essential. Very often the required data is simply not available, and other techniques have to be adopted to simulate the particular risk or risk groupings under consideration. However, even when data is available, a practical difficulty is the correct interpretation of the explanatory descriptions when applying it to anticipated risks on current work.

Just as with project cost estimating, there is no better source of information than an organization's own *historical database*. This should consist of recorded risk events and experience on past projects, preferably of a similar nature where these exist, built up as a result of formalized post-project assessments described below.

2. Current Project Database

If a project is already in the implementation phase, every effort should be made to collect appropriate ongoing data to establish a *current project database* of frequently recurring risk, as the project proceeds. This will be particularly valuable for updating the assessment of overall project risk.

However, for many of the risks, especially at the initial impact analysis stage, the data are necessarily subjective in nature and must be obtained through lessons learned by others, or by careful questioning of experts or persons with the relevant knowledge. For example, an expert could be asked to estimate the optimistic, most probable and pessimistic values for a particular variable, together with explanation of the factors which might contribute to the degree of variability represented in these estimates. The amount at stake for each and the sensitivity of this amount to changes in related variables must also be determined.

3. Post-Project Review and Archive

The compilation of useful historical data is quite a challenging task. It is a task which may be set aside unless its value is recognized and the data collected and organized as part of the project's ongoing management responsibility. The descriptions of risk assessments, events experienced and their consequences should all be recorded.

Consistently structured *post-project reviews* or evaluations in which planning assumptions are matched with actual experience, variances conscientiously explained, and the overall success of the project thoroughly assessed, are essential to consistently good project management. All essential data associated with risk management, systematically collected, carefully structured, and accurately recorded while each project is ongoing, should also be included in the post-project review.

The key elements of each post-project review should then be abstracted and appropriately archived to update the organization's historical database. The post-project review and data archiving should be considered as part of the project's termination phase and completed before its conclusion. Such documentation can be quite a demanding technical responsibility.

---

1. *PMBOK*, 3/28/87, pE-4.

Chapter VII   Management of Contingency Allowances

A. After the Known Risks, What Then?

So far this handbook has dealt with the identification of project risks and how they can be evaluated. That's fine for the risks that can be identified, the known-unknowns. But what about the unknown-unknowns, should they be ignored? Maybe, it's a question of interpretation. Given the definition of unknown-unknowns in Chapter III.C, it is simply not possible to plan for unknown-unknowns.

The 1973 Arab oil embargo is a good example of an unknown-unknown. Cost estimates which were prepared prior to the embargo contained no provisions for such increased fuel costs—no estimator could have possibly been expected to foresee that problem. In other words, in looking into the future, *there is absolutely no way that unknown-unknowns can be taken into account*. We must simply take our lumps as they materialize.[1]

However, problems do surface on projects which are "unexpected" and are tagged with the inference of being unknown-unknowns simply because they were not thought of during planning (even though they should have been!). In reality, they are known-unknowns whose existence and degree of impact on the project are uncertain. Experiencing "unexpected" events may be a reflection of weaknesses in the original planning assumptions.

Planning assumption weaknesses may include:

- Predictions that prove to be false or overstated,
- Lack of timely information for project performance,
- Loss of control during project realization,
- Human resources that are not available when required,
- Lack of competence in key individuals or workforce,
- Disruption due to personal conflicts or internal politics, or simply,
- The occurrence of misunderstandings, burn-out and sickness.

Any such weaknesses should be carefully examined and accounted for by suitable mitigating steps, contingency plans, work-arounds, or otherwise accommodated from allowances for identified risks. If, however, the impact is greater than can be so accommodated, then the project manager may well have to negotiate a change in the scope or quality of the work, take more time, spend more money, or some of all four, in order to complete the project. If a situation develops which is beyond recall, then the project should be aborted as promptly as possible to minimize further wasted time and effort.

B. Contingency Reserves?

From the foregoing discussion it would appear to be prudent to hold some contingency reserves, where this is permissible, to cover unexpected needs on the part of the project sponsor, principally in scope and quality requirements, which will surface in both the time and cost dimensions. However, the existence of any such allowances and their proper management present the project sponsor, and indeed the project manager, with some difficult philosophical and psychological management choices. For example: should they be added to the estimates of time and cost of the project? Or should some flexibility be permitted in the accomplishment of the scope and quality of the project instead?

Neither the client nor the project manager relishes having to make changes to the project's constraints once they have been agreed upon. Wise project managers negotiate time and cost allowances in their plans from the beginning to provide them with some management flexibility. Sometimes this flexibility can be effectively accomplished by identifying some peripheral or minor scope objectives that are not mandatory. Such flexibility greatly enhances the project manager's ability to exercise influence in managing the project.

If time and cost reserves are set aside, should they be under the control of the project's sponsor, the project manager, or the functional managers? Should they be global like big pots to be dipped into when needed, or should they be allocated on some basis appropriate to authority and responsibility on the project? And finally, having regard to the propensity for any spare time and money to be spent, often well before the project is even completed, should such allowances be public or secret?

A prudent sponsor will hold some schedule and financial reserves for the sponsor's own needs, and the project manager may or may not be aware of their existence. An "unsophisticated" client, on the other hand, may not know enough to have them, so the project manager should not count on access to any "secret" reserves.

In practice, the answers to these issues probably lie in the strength and experience of the project's sponsor, management, and general culture surrounding the project. What these questions do point to, however, is the importance of applying risk management, first to reduce project risks to an acceptable minimum, and then to justify effective cost and schedule contingency allowances to cover the remainder. It will be up to project management to properly manage and control these allowances for the ultimate success of the project.

C. Application of Project Contingency Allowances

Contingency allowances are different, separate, and in addition to the schedule and financial resources determined by good estimating techniques. Good estimating requires stating the estimating strategy, the planning assumptions and the typical risks included.

For example, when using a probabilistic estimating technique, particularly when a range of any type is associated with the cost, the given range is actually a "basic contingency" allowance, both positive and negative, for that cost. Basic contingency is designed to cover the inherent variability in the cost of the given element. For that reason, in probabilistic estimates, no additional "basic contingency" should be added at the bottom of the estimate. That would be accounting for it twice.[2]

Separate from the "basic contingency" issue, there may be a need to consider other types of allowance to cover recognized scope uncertainties, resource uncertainties, and so on. An actual contingency amount is then derived from these adjustments which are needed to bring the project's probability of overrun or underrun to an acceptable level. Such allowances should be applied just once—at the "bottom line" of the estimate. They should not be duplicated or "layered" as a result of various estimate segments being combined to form larger segments. Otherwise, the accumulated total may be excessive and make the overall project plan too long, too costly, or both.[3]

D. Contingency Allowances for Project Implementation

Strategies for handling contingencies in the implementation phase of a project, that is, after the *go/no-go decision*, will likely depend on the type of project, its criticality, and whether it is being conducted with resources internal or external to the organization. In any case, for effective schedule and cost control during project implementation, a realistic project schedule and budget must be approved as the baseline terms of reference. This approval normally depends on the schedule and cost estimates submitted as part of the output of the project's development and planning phase.

For purposes of the following illustrations, we will look at the stages of a construction industry project. Approaches to other types of projects should be adjusted accordingly. It will be assumed that the project will be realized substantially by external resources under contract. If this is not the case, then the approach should be modified to suit the particular in-house policies and procedures of the sponsoring organization in question. For our purposes in arriving at appropriate schedule and cost contingency allowances for the implementation phase, this phase may be viewed as having three stages as follows:[4]

1. **Before contract award.** In this stage, after approval to proceed with the project but before award of any work to contractors, it will be necessary to establish the scope and quality of work

required in as much detail as possible. This is typically conveyed by means of scope of work descriptions, designs and specifications. This work itself may be the subject of contracts, if not performed internally. Either way, the quality of this work is critical to subsequent success and requires sound project management, with regular reviews until the product of this stage is satisfactory.

2. **Contract award.** This is the procurement, tendering and award stage. When placing an order or contract, especially if firm price bids are being sought, a variance will inevitably exist between the estimates developed pre-tender and the schedules and prices submitted. This is due to market pressures at the time of bidding, such as service and material price fluctuations, impending labor agreements or disputes, productivity assessments, and whether contractors are busy or slack and their consequent attitude to risk.

3. **After contract award.** It is in this stage, the main production stage, that the various unforeseen items really emerge. Typically, this is evidenced by the necessity for issuing change instructions. Any change will have a disruptive effect on the work. The more changes, and the later they are, the more disruptive to schedule and cost will be their effect.

In many ways, the number of changes that are necessary after contract award will be a reflection of how well the planning was done prior to award, or the detailing of the work earlier in the current phase. Of course, the sponsoring organization may have set a deliberate policy of awarding contracts before all the information is complete in order to reduce the overall time for the project. This project management strategy is often referred to as "fast-tracking," and puts the project into a much higher risk category. Under these circumstances, appropriate contingency allowances must be increased accordingly.

E. Implementation Contingency Strategies

Typical approaches to setting contingencies vary from applying standard allowances, to percentages based on past experience, to a careful assessment based on the sum total of the most likely probability and consequences of the various risk items properly identified.[5] It is the latter which is being advocated in this handbook, as part of a pro-active and responsible approach to project risk management. A simple format is described in Section F.

In fact, the first two approaches may be characterized as the "big pot" approach. When anything goes wrong, everyone dips into the big pot. Unfortunately, the pot always seems to be emptied long before the project is completed. Indeed, the reality is exacerbated by the perception, because people are tempted to raid the pot before it is too late!

It is true that when a contingency allowance is based on probability and severity of occurrence and is allocated to each item proportionately, no single amount is sufficient to cover its corresponding risk event. The concept is based on probability "swings-and-roundabouts" and so it is most important to establish policies and procedures for managing the complete contingency allowance.

A recommended approach is that once appropriate allowances have been determined, allocations should be made to the major functional areas of responsibility associated with each of the three implementation stages described in Section D. Table VII.1 shows a matrix chart for a construction project in which allocations have been made to each of these three stages and to each of four functional areas of responsibility.

Table VII.1. Contingency Allocation: Construction Project

RESPONSIBILITY	STAGE		
	PRE-AWARD	AWARD	POST-AWARD
OWNER	Policy Changes Scope Changes 1 % Enhancements (All nominal)		Policy Changes Scope Changes Enhancements 1/2% Budget and Cash Flow Difficulties
MANAGER	Schedule Delays 1 %	Tendering Variances 5 % Market Conditions Inflation	Other Contractors 1/2% Equipment Delivery
DESIGNER	Re-evaluation of Design Design Changes 1 %		Coordination "Making it Work" 1/2%
CONTRACTOR			Changed Conditions Claims for Delays 1/2% Inflation Legal Interpretation

In the example, suppose a total contingency cost allowance of 10 percent for the implementation phase has been arrived at. Then, say, 1 percent might be allocated to each of the sponsor, project manager and designers in the pre-award stage for a total of 3 percent, and 5 percent allowance assigned to the award stage. This leaves 2 percent for the post-award stage, plus whatever is carried forward from the two earlier stages. This latter carry forward is justified as follows:

Assuming that the original estimate is reasonably sound, and that firm price tenders have been called for, then if the market conditions are depressed, very competitive bids may be received. This could mean that little, if any, of the award stage allowance is consumed; indeed, it might even be enhanced. However, it is then appropriate to increase the post-award stage contingency allowances because the probability of contract administration difficulties and consequent claims arising is correspondingly increased.

Of the three stages described, contract award is probably the most uncertain. For example, in construction work, even under good bidding conditions and on a "good set of documents," the core bids (i.e., those bids not containing gross estimating or computation errors or extremes) are likely to vary at least by 5 percent to 10 percent, simply as a result of differences in production methods, productivity assumptions and required margins. However, if the bids are scattered well beyond this range, perhaps the documents should be re-examined for ambiguity or lack of clarity and precision.

F. A Simple Tabular Calculation

A simple computation to arrive at an appropriate estimating contingency allowance to cover the consequences of second- and lower-order risks may be arrived at by using the tabular format shown in Table VII.2

Table VII.2. Simple Tabular Calculation of Estimating Contingency

Description of Risk Event	Probability of Occurrence	Estimated Cost of Consequence (Amount at Stake)	Risk Event Status (Criterion Value) $
Risk Event #1	Probability P	Cost C	PxC
Risk Event #2	do.	do.	do.
etc.	do.	do.	do.
Project Estimating Contingency based on:			Σ PxC

This exercise itself may well identify higher-than-reasonable risks requiring risk management focus. All first-order risks, i.e., those with both a high probability and high amount-at-stake should, of course, be reported to senior management or the project sponsor for appropriate action. Depending on that decision, and the degree of controllability of the particular risk, it may be necessary for project management to establish a disclaimer regarding the consequences.

In summary, effective contingency management requires a positive and systematic approach. By doing so, changes in the status of the allowances and, hence, the trends in the final position at the end of the project will be very good indicators of its health. Moreover, adverse trends can be brought to the attention of those who are able to significantly influence the future course of events in the interests of the project's ultimate success.

1. M.W. Curran, Decision Sciences Corporation, in letter dated November 26, 1990.
2. Ibid.
3. A.M. Ruskin and W.E. Estes, *What Every Engineer Should Know about Project Management*, Marcel Dekker, Inc., New York, 1982, p45.
4. R.M. Wideman, Cost Control of Capital Projects, A.E.W. Services, Vancouver, B.C., 1983, p75.
5. Ibid., p76.

Chapter VIII   Managing the Risks of the Project's Environment

A. What is the Project Environment?

Why worry about the project environment...when the objective of project management is to get the project completed within scope, cost and schedule? The truth is that what is ultimately at risk is *project success*, so important though these objective criteria are, they are not necessarily the ultimate determinants of success. Heresy? Perhaps. But success, a very elusive notion at best, is dependent upon navigating the project through all its various uncertainties (risks) and ending up with satisfied customers.

Who are the customers? In varying degrees, just about anyone involved with the project, in other words, the project stakeholders. It is these stakeholders collectively who establish the various cultures surrounding the project and thereby establish the project's environment. Two views of the project environment are shown conceptually in Figures VIII.1 and 2. The following discussion

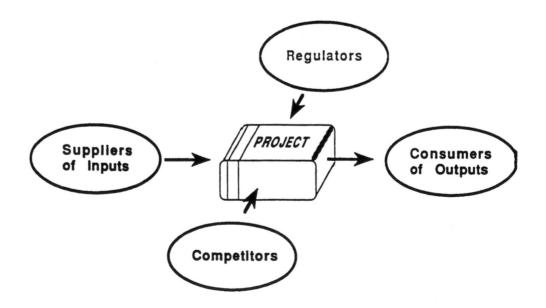

Figure VIII.1. Project Environment Process

After N.R. Burnett and R. Youker, EDI Training Course, CN-848, July 1980.

Figure VIII.2. Project Environment: External Influences and Interfaces
R.M. Wideman, Project Management Course, 1990

looks at the environment from the perspective of risk. For convenience, this environment may be thought of in terms of the internal project culture, the sponsors' (permanent) corporate culture, and the external social surroundings.

The internal and corporate stakeholders are the easiest to recognize, and the manager of the successful project understands the need to be attuned to current organizational, social and political maneuverings to avoid some classic project risks. To advantage, he or she may spend some time and effort in influencing these environments for the benefit of project team performance. For example, every project team member needs to be convinced of the project's worth and become dedicated towards its objectives. Top management needs to be convinced of the benefits of appropriate training, and its power in developing competence and commitment. In this way, misunderstandings, mistakes, and rework may be avoided, and the consequences of such risks correspondingly reduced.

B. Problems are Caused by People

The external stakeholders are more difficult to identify and include all those who will in any way be involved with the resulting entity or product upon its completion. Typically, that's a lot of people, and today there is a rapidly growing awareness and concern amongst them for the impacts on their physical environment.

This is particularly true of hard, commercial and industrial, projects, but it is also often true of soft, administrative-type projects, and the subsequent stress in the working environment. The problem is that people are understandably resistant to change because the known is always more comfortable than the unknown. For example, when a situation has remained stable for a significant period, individuals develop all sorts of habits and short-cuts that work to their personal advantage. Change threatens to destroy this personal comfort base, forcing people to start afresh. These vested interests, together with an initial lack of understanding and a perception that there will be winners and losers, all too often constitute serious hurdles to be overcome. Yet too frequently these very hurdles are simply overlooked during the course of the project.

This resistance to change may be evident amongst many of the stakeholders. Others may simply have counter vested interests, or personal or group agendas, which are only indirectly related to the project. Together with the project's sponsors, owners and users, these people constitute the project's direct and indirect stakeholders. Collectively or separately, their attitudes and expectations may well undermine the success of the project.

This leads to the possibility of influencing these attitudes and expectations in such a way that the change which the project is designed to introduce will be much better received. If these uncertainties can be uncovered in good time, they can be dealt with pro-actively so that the corresponding risks to the project are significantly reduced.

C. Risk and Safety[1]

A good example of the potential for attitudes to undermine a project is public concern over safety and/or environmental damage. An organization may have a finely tuned project risk management program in place, and still suddenly find itself in the middle of an hysterical local community distraught over public fears and media distortion of a risk issue. The fact is, risk management is not complete without effective risk communications. Suggested mechanisms for public communication are outlined in Sections E and F below, but perhaps it is worthwhile discussing at this point why traditional responses with factual data tend to fail.

Research into the psychology of risk perceptions by U.S. psychologists Paul Slovic and Vince Covello indicates:

1. People do not, in fact, demand zero risk. They take risks every day, both consciously and subconsciously, and they are willing and able to take benefit/risk decisions, as in driving and speeding. Some take deliberate risks simply for pleasure, prestige or self-satisfaction (e.g., sky diving).
2. Peoples' judgments of degrees of risk are not, however, coincident with most methodologies for measuring risk statistically. The public may greatly underestimate familiar risks

(e.g., driving) while greatly overestimating unfamiliar risks (e.g., buying a home near a nuclear facility).

3. A variety of emotional, not logical, factors control risk perceptions:

    • Primary is the sense of *personal control,* i.e., the ability to *choose* taking a risk (like getting into a car) and the ability to *manage* the risk (I am the one behind the wheel).
    • Secondary are qualities of familiarity and, conversely, dread. The greater the unfamiliarity and potential for connection to gruesome (e.g., nuclear impacts), the more it is likely to be judged as highly risky and therefore unacceptable.

4. Once established, risk perceptions are extremely hard to change. New information may be absorbed by the intellect but it is not readily absorbed at an emotional level.
5. Risk perceptions reside fundamentally at an emotional level.

What these insights suggest is that, in a crisis of fear, the traditional management instinct of providing rational, statistically-based information could be misguided.

In a recent egg/salmonella case, spokesmen for the egg producers tried to explain the extremely low risks of an individual actually being made sick by an infected egg. What they failed to recognize was the sanctity of food and the trust in those who deliver it. It is not a question of how much risk, but rather the sudden imposition without warning of risk into a system assumed to be low- risk. As a result, the problem effectively got out of control.

In the example, risk communications should have tried to address the issues of *surprise events* and *loss of control.* Instead of trying to prove that there was "no problem, except for the elderly, the infirm and babies," a better response might have been "A detailed examination has been ordered to determine the extent to which the problem exists. We will get to the bottom of it and keep you fully informed. For the moment we recommend that all eggs be thoroughly cooked, and that the elderly, infirm and small children limit their consumption. Anyone with these symptoms should immediately call, etc., etc."

The difference in the two approaches is that the first assumes that there is a basis of trust, or fails to recognize the need to establish a basis for trust by asking people to be reasonable. The second endeavors to establish a basis of trust by showing that the problem is being actively monitored and controlled.

If the research demonstrates that the fundamentals of risk perception are emotional and not rational, then the primary focus of project risk management communications should be to establish (or re-establish) trust in the organization, rather than to educate the public about science or technology and its benefits. This means beginning by recognizing the natural legitimacy of public emotional response to risk, and responding by seeking a change in the attitude towards those who are being held responsible for creating and managing the risk. This is in contrast to seeking a change in the perception of the risk itself.

D. Principal Determinants

To identify the potential difficulties associated with project risks and to assess their probability of occurrence, designated members of the project team must interact frequently with those institutions and individuals which constitute the most important elements of the project's stakeholders. The required effort can then be priorized with a view to heading off the most serious obstacles well in advance.

This environment will not be the same for every project, of course. In fact, it is likely to be determined principally by three considerations:[2]

- The product or service resulting from the project,
- The technology and the manner of its application, and
- Its physical location.

Suggested steps in the process of identification are:[3]

1. Learn how to understand the role of the various stakeholders, and how this information may be used as an opportunity to improve both the perception and reception of the project.
2. Identify the real nature of each stakeholder group's business and their consequent interest in the project.
3. Understand their motivation and behavior.
4. Assess how they may react to various approaches.
5. Pinpoint the characteristics of the stakeholders' environment and develop appropriate responses to facilitate a good relationship.
6. Learn project management's role in responding to the stakeholders' drive behind the project.
7. Determine the key areas which will have the most impact on the successful reception of the project by all the stakeholders.
8. Develop a Project Acceptance Plan aimed at managing external stakeholders' interests.

However, remember always that even a minor stakeholder group may discover that "fatal flaw" in the project's concept that could bring it to a standstill! Failure to deal with these issues in a timely manner will inevitably lead to a less than optimum project outcome.

E. Managing by Stakeholder Groupings and Categories

Project stakeholders may be recognized in any of the following categories:[4]

- Those who are directly related to the project by having a stake in its process or product such as suppliers of inputs, managers of the process, or consumers of outputs;

- Those who have influence over the physical, infrastructural, technological, commercial/financial/socioeconomic, or political/legal conditions;
- Those who have a hierarchical relationship to the project such as government authorities at local, regional and national levels; and
- Those individuals, groups or associations, sometimes only indirectly related to the project, but who see a linkage between their own interests and the project's goals and who pursue it for their own ends. These may include special interest groups or competitors, but also those providing services who wish to profit at the expense of the project.

Having identified the various stakeholder groupings, each may be assigned to a category according to their amenability to influence. Three categories are suggested, namely:

- Those who are controllable,
- Those who are influenceable, and
- Those who need to be appreciated.

Within each category, stakeholders may then be further rated by degree of importance according to their ability to influence the outcome of the project. Members of the project team can then prioritize their efforts to maintain effective stakeholder linkages, designed to give the best chances of ultimate project success.

Possibly the largest constituency are those who are relatively neutral at the outset and can therefore be influenced in their opinion. They may also represent the best source of potential support and hence the best opportunity to establish a perception of project success, if their opinion is mobilized effectively. If the project is sufficiently large or visible, a separate program of effort may be assigned to a specific group as a special *public relations* (PR) effort.

Either way, the trick is to persuade the various players that what they want is the same as the project's objectives, or else to modify the project's objectives accordingly. The goal is to establish such a congruence through risk management.

F. The Means and Value of Exercising Positive Influence

What are the hallmarks of a successful PR program? Here is a top-ten check list:[5]

- Quality information about the benefits of the project
- Participation in those decisions which have some degree of flexibility, or constitute viable alternatives, and which may result in enhanced project value
- Care and concern genuinely expressed for the project's stakeholders
- Information requirements anticipated and provided ahead of time
- Timely response to other information requests

- Genuinely sincere appreciation expressed to inquirers
- Flexible personal responses provided, where special issues dictate
- Recovery from inevitable lapses of existing services during project activities, in ways that impress
- Project team members empowered to make decisions to solve urgent and obvious local problems
- Stakeholder-friendly information facilities available both during project implementation, as well as subsequently

Traditional management has long since recognized the value of the classic input-process-output model, with its management information feedback loop for controlling output. Dynamic managers have also recognized that opening communication channels in both directions, such that modified management strategies result, can be a particularly powerful workforce motivator. The key is quality information. Whether this information is presented in verbal, written or graphical form, improvements in performance can be quite remarkable and, indeed, many "knowledge workers" demand it to provide them with job satisfaction. The concept is shown in Figure VIII.3.

The principle is just as true in the field of projects, though regretfully less evident, especially where the external environment is concerned. Thus, the project manager's job is no longer confined to controlling events within his or her own organization. It is no longer sufficient to think of project management simply as the monitoring of time and cost by planning, scheduling and resource leveling, as some scheduling software promotion seems to suggest. Nor is it sufficient just to include the many other administrative tasks required of the project manager as leader of the project team.

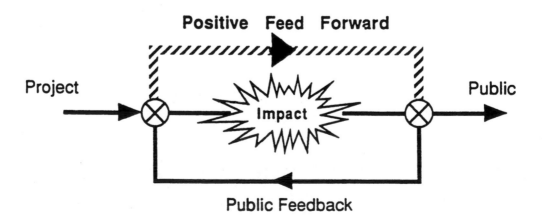

Figure VIII.3. Managing the Environment: Public Relations Concept
R.M. Wideman, Managing the Project Environment,
Dimensions of Project Management, Springer-Verlag, New York, 1990, p63.

Today, to a remarkable extent, the success of a project depends on the ability of the project manager and his or her team to establish a genuine and positive influence over the attitudes of the stakeholders.

A favorable perception means a successful reception!

1. Adapted from J. Lindheim, Distress Signals, *Management Today*, BIM, London, April 1989, p105.
2. Galbraith, 1977.
3. R.M. Wideman, Good Public Relations: An Essential Part of Successful Project Management, PMI Seminar/Symposium Proceedings, Denver, Colorado, 1985.
4. Adapted from Asian Development Bank, Analyzing the Project Environment, 13th ADB Regional Seminar MS, Manila, Philippines, 1987.
5. D.M. Connor, abstracted from promotional literature, Connor Development Services, Victoria, B.C., 1989.

Chapter IX   Dealing with Risks in Contracts

A. Contract Strategy Considerations

Selection of an appropriate procurement strategy will depend upon the type of project, its particular emphasis in terms of scope, quality, time and cost, and the degree of uncertainty associated with each. Careful consideration of these aspects should lead to the right choice of organizational structure, allocation of responsibility, and means of procurement. If the project is to be realized by internal resources, then any commitments will be less formal since they are not "at arms length" in a strictly legal sense even though they may become part of an employment contract. However, any risks arising out of uncertainty under agreements internal to the organization rest with the organization, so the issue is not "contractual" but rather one of internal policies and procedures.

Whenever any work is to be contracted for outside the organization then a suitable contract needs to be formulated in some detail. The manner of its development, tendering or negotiation and award procedures, are the subject of the PMI Handbook on Contract/Procurement. However, a range of types of contract is possible in which the degree of associated risk is shared differently between the parties. The choice of which type of contract is most suited to the project in question is very much the subject of project risk management. The selection of the right form of contract requires:

· The identification of specific risks,
· Determination of how they should be shared between the parties, and
· The insertion of clear legal language in the contract documents to put it into effect.

The most challenging of these tasks is the finding of a cost-effective and equitable degree of risk allocation. Standard contract (or purchase order) documents prepared by various levels of government, organizations which undertake a lot of procurement, or standard model documents prepared for various industry sectors, such as construction, are typically used. Specific allocations of risk are intrinsic to such standard forms, but the principles behind the allocations are rarely stated.[1] Such intrinsic allocation of risk may or may not be appropriate to the project.

B. Suggested Risk Sharing Principles

Various authors have sought to identify principles which should govern the allocation of risk amongst the parties to a project.[2] Recommendations are suggested by the answers to these questions:

- Which party is the source of the particular risk and hence best able to control the events that may lead to it happening in the first place?
- Which party can best manage the risk, if it occurs?
- Is it or is it not preferable for the client to retain an involvement in the management of the risk in question?
- If it cannot be controlled, which party can or should carry the risk?
- Will the cost incurred, or premium charged, by the recipient of the risk be reasonable and cost-effective?
- Will the recipient be capable of sustaining the consequences of the risk, if it occurs?
- Or will it lead to the possibility of other risks of a different nature being transferred back again, e.g., slow down or collapse of the project effort through demoralization or bankruptcy, etc.?

If at the time of entering into a contract the distribution of risk is not clearly understood, or is patently unfair, such as one party being the cause of risks which are then sustained by the other party, then disputes are almost inevitable. The adoption of systematic project risk identification and analysis may consequently result in departing from the standard contract conditions in particular circumstances, to the overall benefit of the project.

SCOPE OF WORK INFORMATION	very little		partial		complete
UNCERTAINTY	high		moderate		low
DEGREE OF RISK	high		medium		low
SUGGESTED RISK ALLOCATION	 100% AGENCY (BUYER) 0%			SELLER (CONTRACTOR)	0% 100%
CONTRACT TYPES	CPPF	CPIF	CPFF	FPPI	FFP

CPPF - Cost Plus Percentage Fee   FPPI - Fixed Price Plus Incentive
CPIF - Cost Plus Incentive Fee   FFP - Firm Fixed Price
CPFF - Cost Plus Fixed Fee

Figure IX.1. Contract Type vs. Risk Allocation

C. Types of Contract

The term *contract* has been defined in various ways by various authorities. Also, the law of contract depends on the jurisdiction, so that the essential attributes of a valid contract may vary. However, for project purposes, two requirements appear to be immutable—in return for a legal act, there shall be legal "consideration." It is the consideration, or form of payment mechanism, which has led to a variety of different contracts.

These different types of contract range from fixed-price-lump-sum for the identified work, to fully cost-reimbursable. While the payment mechanism may be a reflection of the current practice in a particular industry, it is also often a reflection of how much is known beforehand of the work to be accomplished. Work that is fully described, can proceed without interruption and can therefore be scheduled and estimated, is appropriate to a fixed price. Work that is essentially undefined and/or cannot be scheduled is obviously highly uncertain, and therefore risky, and in fact is unlikely to proceed except on some form of cost reimbursable basis. Figure IX.1 shows a typical relationship between different types of contract and the allocation of risk.

In other words, the payment mechanism is a reflection of the degree of uncertainty, i.e., risk. So it transpires that one of the most significant differences between the various forms of contract is the way in which risks are handled and *paid for*, ranging from those which are *price-based* to those which are *cost-based*.

In price-based contracts (i.e., lump sum, and, to a slightly lesser extent, unit price contracts where the quantities of individual units are expected to vary), payment is deemed to cover all costs, overheads and profit, wherein the *contractor* includes all necessary contingencies for risks specified and/or inferred.

Cost-based contracts are at the other end of the scale. Here, all costs actually incurred in the performance of the contract are reimbursed and, in addition, a fee is paid to cover profit and any associated costs and overheads which are not defined as reimbursable. It follows from this arrangement that virtually all risks are paid for by the *client*, unless specified otherwise and covered by the agreed upon fee.

Almost as a corollary to the allocation of risk between these two extremes is the degree to which the owner or client has the opportunity to get involved in the management and organization of the work and to make changes. In the former, management and organization of the work must be in the hands of the contractor with quite rigid procedures for making changes. In the latter, there can be a high degree of flexibility.

At first glance, it might be supposed that the cost-reimbursable approach is the ideal form of contract. Unfortunately, it is the subject of very detailed and accurate cost and progress record keeping, which even then may be the subject of independent audit and dispute. Perhaps more important is the lack of incentive to control cost and schedule by those engaged under the contract.

This has given rise to a whole range of *cost-plus-incentive* types of contract. The range of possibilities tend to be a function of the imagination of the respective contract negotiators and seem to be almost endless. In any case, this is the subject of Contract/Procurement Management. Suffice it to repeat here that the particular form of contract adopted will be a reflection of the degree of uncertainty, and how the risks are to be allocated and paid for.

D. Different Contract Risk Implications

Figure IX.2 shows probability curve distributions for three projects all with the same expected value. However, the probability of project A being completed for this value is the highest compared to projects B and C because it has the best definition of scope of work. The figure also suggests the type of contract appropriate to the range of uncertainty.

Table IX.1 shows the impact of different issues on the different types of contract.[3] It also shows how risk may be distributed or handled in each case.

E. More Than One Contract

In many project situations, more than a single implementation contract is involved. In program management, for example, there will be a series of projects, running either consecutively or concurrently which will no doubt involve separate contracts. Or within a project, particularly one which is complex, large, and/or

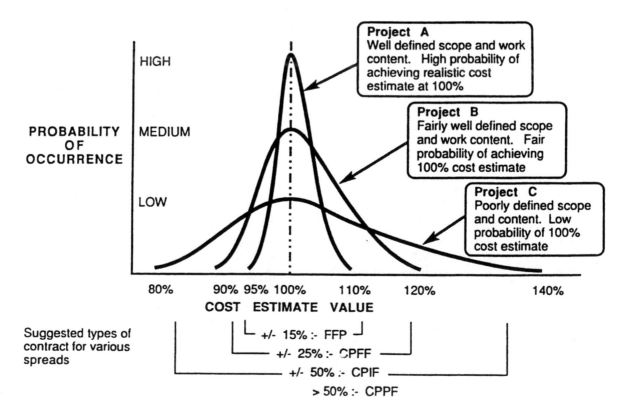

Figure IX.2. Scope Definition - Risk - Contract Selection

Table IX.1. Risk Implications of Different Types of Contract (from Client's perspective)

Issue	Type of Contract			
	Lump Sum	Unit Price	Target Cost	Cost Reimbursable
Financial objectives of client and contractor	Different but reasonably independent	Different and in potential conflict	Considerable harmony. Reduction of actual cost is a common objective provided cost remains within the incentive region	Both based on actual cost but in potential conflict
Contractor's involvement in design	Excluded if competitive price based on full design and specifications	Usually excluded	Contractor encouraged to contribute ideas for reducing cost	Contractor may be appointed for design input prior to execution
Client involvement in management of execution	Excluded	Virtually excluded	Possible through joint planning	Should be active involvement
Claims resolution	Very difficult, no basis for $$ evaluation	Difficult, only limited basis for $$ evaluation	Potentially easy, based on actual costs. Contract needs careful drafting	Unnecessary except for fee adjustment. Usually relatively easy
Forecast final cost at time of bid	Known, except for unknown claims and changes	Uncertain, depending on quantity variations and unknown claims and changes	Uncertain. Target cost usually increased by changes, but effective joint management and efficient working can reduce final cost below an original realistic budget	Unknown
Payment for cost of risk events	Depending on contract terms, undisclosed contingency, if any, in contractor's bid. Otherwise by claim and negotiation	Depending on contract terms, undisclosed contingency, if any, in contractor's bid. Otherwise by claim and negotiation	Payment of actual cost of dealing with risks as they occur, and target adjusted accordingly	Payment of actual costs

organized on a specialty or trade basis, there may be numerous separate service agreements and contracts to be coordinated.

The work involved in the different phases and stages of the project may also be the subject of different contracts or agreements. For example, in the project development phase, social, environmental, market and technical studies may be procured from different specialists. Even a separate risk analysis study may be commissioned for a large or critical project. In subsequent stages detailed specification, design and supervision or quality control and expediting may be the subject of separate specialized packages, and so on.

The greater the number of separate packages under separate and discrete responsibilities, the greater the amount of coordination required and the greater the resulting risk. Consequently, early in the development of the project the project sponsor must develop a suitable contract strategy and establish an organizational structure consistent with the intended project objectives. The organizational structure selected must reflect the proper division of responsibility for these various components in terms of scope, quality, time and cost, including any delegation of project management responsibility. The strategy must recognize the need for management coordination and integration of the various contracts over time by making corresponding provisions in each of the contracts.

There are many different ways of structuring a project's procurement to suit differing objectives and circumstances. Different structures assign risk in different ways. Perhaps the most significant issue for project risk management is the overall distribution of responsibility for project risk as reflected by:

· The ways in which management responsibility is structured,
· How it is delegated, and
· How it is incorporated into the various contracts.

Responsibility for the costs of risk events for different types of typical standard contract is also compared in Table IX.1.

F. A Question of Attitudes

Many descriptions of successful projects (e.g. Showcase Projects reported in the *PM NETwork*) reflect on the healthy cooperative team spirit enjoyed on the project. So it is not necessarily the project organizational structure and forms of contract which determine whether or not project objectives are successfully achieved, but rather the attitudes of the parties involved. However, an effective structure and good contract wording can go a long way to establish good relations and avoid the frustrations which otherwise undermine initial enthusiasm and good intentions.

Obviously, this includes an equitable distribution of risk, and the means for handling it in the event that it arises. Suggested characteristics of good contract conditions in respect of risk include:[4]

- Clear definitions of risk and their assignment
- Positive incentives linked to risk assignment
- Flexibility for different assignment of different risks between parties
- Strong emphasis on good management practices designed to avoid unnecessary risks

Handling project risk in the way described may require a departure from sometimes traditional forms of contract. However, if the effect is to avoid or reduce the number of contract disputes, as well as the amounts of money under dispute, then the respective levels of management will have more time to spend on the real issue—project success.

1. R.W. Hayes et al, Risk Management in Engineering Construction, Special SERC Report by the Project Management Group, UMIST, Thomas Telford Ltd., London, December 1986.
2. Ibid., p26. Other authors include D.B. Ashley, C.E. Porter, N.M.L. Barnes, J.G. Perry and P.A. Thompson, p30. See also Contract Risk Allocation and Cost Effectiveness, CII Publication 5-3, Austin, Texas, November 1988.
3. After R.W. Hayes et al, Risk Management in Engineering Construction, Special SERC Report by the Project Management Group, UMIST, Thomas Telford Ltd., London, December 1986, p29.
4. Ibid., p28.

Chapter X   Summary/Conclusions

A. Risk Management - The Present

Projects are launched to take advantage of opportunities, but opportunities are associated with uncertainties which have risks attached. For the project to be viable, the expected value resulting from a favorable probability of gain must be higher than the consequences and probability of loss. Therefore, the risks associated with a project must receive careful examination in the context of the organization's willingness or aversion to taking risks. This is the domain of Project Risk Management, which forms a vital part of Project Management.

With careful planning and good management some inherent risks in the project management process can be substantially reduced or virtually eliminated. Steps towards this goal include:

- Thorough and realistic appraisal of the project concept, and hence scope definition, in the concept phase
- Observing good project management practices in the project planning and development phase, including realistic estimating of time and cost for defined scope and quality
- Examining the uncertainty and risk inherent in the project, and identifying ways of mitigation, and/or making due contingency allowances where the scope of work is uncertain
- Preparing contingent action plans and work-arounds
- Developing sound procurement strategies designed to optimize performance, supported by an appropriate organizational structure and responsibility distribution
- Assigning specific responsibility for risk in a way that motivates by recognizing that risk and reward go together
- Examining contract documents for risk identification, general clarity and potential sources of misunderstanding
- Seeking innovative but practical solutions to offset potential areas of risk

While many of the details described in the foregoing chapters of this handbook are applicable to large complex projects, the principles involved are just as applicable to any size of project in any field of endeavor. Since there is no point in taking any risk that has negative expected value, the principles of risk management should be an established part of early project management activities on all projects—whether complex or simple, large or small.

B. It's the Attitude That Counts

Successful projects such as Showcase Projects reported in the *PM NETwork* emphasize the benefits of a healthy cooperative project team spirit and constructive attitude. Appropriate procurement strategies, project organizational structure, responsibility distribution and corresponding forms of contract should all be designed to support this positive attitude towards successfully achieving project objectives. Effective and equitable handling of project risks can go a long way towards establishing such good relations and avoiding the frustrations which otherwise undermine initial enthusiasm and good intentions.

C. Risk Management - The Future?

Because risk has a natural complexity in its variety, scenario combination possibilities and variation in probability impacts unique to each project, there are some ideal opportunities for computer applications. Obvious applications include rapid access to established databases, data storage, repetitive computations ranging from simple to complex, and sensitivity or "what-if" analyses.

However, effective project risk management is also subject to practical experience and sound judgments. Artificial intelligence (AI), expert systems (ES), and, more recently, human-computer cooperative systems (HCCS) are being developed to incorporate these added dimensions. The intent is to enhance the project manager's risk management ability to arrive at better solutions than would have been arrived at without such support systems, e.g., by reducing the recurrence of similar risks.

The ultimate potential of AI and ES (and HCCS) is in their ability to augment the program manager's reasoning power. But to do this a better understanding of cognition, knowledge representation, information usage, effective decision making and risk assessment is still needed.[1]

---

1. M.D. Martin et al, Critical Issues in the Application of Artificial Intelligence (AI) to Acquisition Management, Forum on Artificial Intelligence in Management, Dayton, Ohio, 1988.

Appendix A

Typical Project Risks

1. How Does the Project Manager Know When There is a Project Risk?[1]

Some of the most common general project risk situations encountered:

- The project sponsor (and the project manager) do not recognize that every project is an exercise in risk.
- This project is very different from the last one.
- There is a feeling of uneasiness.
- When the project is in its earliest phase, project risk and opportunity are highest (but the amount-at-stake is lowest).
- The project scope, objectives and deliverables are not clearly defined or understood.
- A large number of alternatives are perceived as possible.
- Some or all technical data is lacking.
- The technical process (and design) are not mature.
- Standards for performance are unrealistic (the best there is for everything) or are absent.
- Costs, schedules and performance are not expressed in ranges.
- The future timing of activities and events are vague.
- Design lacks production engineering input.
- Prototype of a key element is missing.
- There is a higher than usual R&D component.
- Some or all environmental permits are outstanding.
- Other similar projects have been delayed or cancelled.
- A wide variation in bids are received.
- Some key subsystems and/or materials are sole source.
- No appropriate contingency plans have been developed.
- The project team relies entirely on the contingency allowance.
- Someone starts "hedging their bets"!

2. Specific Project Risks

The following detailed listings provide convenient groupings of project risks generally classified according to source. The degree of predictability and ability to manage appropriate response varies but, in any case, is independent of the risk event status (probability and amount at stake).

External Unpredictable (and uncontrollable)

a. Regulatory, i.e., unanticipated government intervention in:
   - supply of raw materials
   - environmental issues
   - design standards
   - production standards
   - site location
   - product or service sales or export
   - pricing
   - special requirements

b. Natural Hazards, i.e., as a result of natural elements:
   - location
   - storm
   - flood
   - earthquake

c. Postulated Events, i..e., as a result of deliberate intent:
   - vandalism
   - sabotage

d. Indirect Effects, i.e., occurring as a result of the project:
   - environmental
   - social

e. Completion, i.e., failure to complete the project on account of one of the following:
   - failure of the supporting infrastructure as a result of others
   - failure of design, execution or supply contracts due to bankruptcy or receivership, etc.
   - failure to provide financial support to the end of the project
   - inappropriate project concept or configuration
   - political unrest
   - lack of final acceptance

External Predictable (but uncontrollable)

Changes in the following are predictable, but the extent and direction is uncertain.

a. Market Risks
   - availability of raw materials
   - cost of raw materials
   - demand, including customer/user rejection
   - economics
   - competition
   - end value in the market
   - willingness of buyers to honor purchase agreements

b. Operational (i.e., after project completion)
   - maintenance needs
   - fitness for purpose
   - safety

c. Environmental Impacts

d. Social Impacts

e. Currency Changes

f. Inflation

g. Taxation

Internal, Non-Technical (but generally controllable)

     a. Management, i.e., difficulties due to:
- insincerity/lack of integrity
- incapacity
- inadequacies
- loss of control
- incompatibility of goals
- senior staff changes
- inappropriate or lack of organizational structure
- lack of appropriate policies and procedures
- inadequate planning
- unrealistic scheduling
- lack of coordination
- inadequate project management

     b. Schedule, i.e., delays and time overrun due to:
- delays due to management difficulties above
- regulatory approvals
- labor shortages
- labor productivity
- labor stoppages
- material shortages
- late deliveries
- unforeseen site conditions
- sponsor/user scope changes
- accident or sabotage
- start-up, turn-over or launch difficulties
- lack of access

     c. Cost, i.e., overruns due to:
- any of the schedule delays listed above
- inappropriate procurement strategy
- pay negotiations
- management and/or workforce inexperience
- lack of understanding how parts fit together
- contractor claims
- under-estimating
- any of the external factors listed previously

     d. Cash Flow
- squeezing
- interruption
- insolvency

     e. Loss of Potential, i.e., removal of:
- benefit
- profit

Technical (and generally controllable)

     a. Changes in Technology
- rendering parts of the project obsolete
- parts discontinued
- introduced by competitors, rendering the project obsolete, uncompetitive, or unacceptable
- complexity introduced as a result of new technology

      b. Performance
- quality
- rate of production
- reliability

      c. Risks Specific to Project's Technology
- in creating the entity or product
- in operating or marketing it

      d. Design
- inadequate data
- designer/detailer inexperience
- design inadequacies
- detail, precision and suitability of the specification
- likelihood of changes during the course of the project
- design vs. execution methods

      e. Sheer size or complexity of project

Legal (generally controllable)

Difficulties arising from any of the following:

a. Licences

b. Patent Rights

c. Contractual i.e., difficulties due to:
- misinterpretation
- misunderstanding
- inappropriate contracting strategy/contract type
- failure

d. Outsider Suit

e. Insider Suit

f. Force Majeure

---

1. After D.T. Hulett, PMP Certification Workshop - Risk Management, PMI Orange County
    Chapter, 1991, p22.

Appendix B

Impact Analysis Methodology

This appendix describes a risk analysis methodology[1] which can be applied to the general situation of managing a project under varying degrees of uncertainty. A risk of the complexity discussed here has generally been applied only to very large programs or projects, such as utility or infrastructure construction. The methodology is described for purposes of illustration.

This type of risk evaluation should typically be carried out very early in the project life cycle. In fact, it should be carried out when real information is most lacking, precisely because it is at this time that a risk analysis can be of most use to the project team in gaining an understanding of the project itself.

However, in order to achieve these benefits, the risk management process should be part of the central project management planning, not merely an optional adjunct. The benefits will be greatest when the project team perceives risk management as a means to project ends, and not an end in itself. The depth of the process can be tailored to suit the size, nature and circumstances of the project.

The methodology which follows is not confined to front-end planning. It can be used equally well for more detailed analyses during subsequent project phases. In fact, the risk framework or models developed in the process can form a valuable baseline for subsequent detailed studies in later stages of the project. Although like most other project management functions the process of risk analysis is iterative, for simplicity it is described as a set of six tasks in the following typical sequence:

1. **Problem Structuring** – confirming the specific objectives of the study, and developing a framework for the analysis.
2. **Risk Identification** – identifying a comprehensive set of risk items associated with project activities incorporating judgments from many sources, initial screening of risk events as to potential risk status, and developing preliminary risk models.
3. **Risk Quantification** – estimating the probability of risk events and the impacts on variables of concern such as performance, delivery, cost, reliability and impact on the project environment.
4. **Risk Modeling** – modeling the combined effects of risks within and between activities, discussing results leading to base plan adjustments for the project as appropriate, and re-running.

5. **Overall Economic Modeling** – producing overall measures of variability in project economics or effectiveness as a result of incorporating the impacts of all risks considered.
6. **Project Risk Report** – presenting the findings and recommendations.

These steps are more particularly described below.

1. Problem Structuring

Perhaps the most important steps in the process, as with any study, is to obtain agreement on the objective and a study plan for its achievement. For example, the objective might simply be stated as *To identify responses appropriate to project risks which may impact project scope, quality, time and/or cost.*

The resulting study plan would then involve steps, firstly, to capture the base case project scope statement in terms of project configuration, with potential project alternatives. Secondly, initiatives would be designed to force discussion of project uncertainties and risks amongst members of the project team to improve the understanding of the project. Thirdly, would be the tasks involved in the structuring of information and analyses required to support the decision making for the project implementation plan.

The information itself will consist of two types: objective and subjective. The objective information may be based on projecting today's understanding and circumstances, be derived from a similar project, be the result of statistical inference, and may lead to a large number of trails. The subjective information may have to be based on a similar project but different assumptions, different projects, limited observations, expert opinion, or mere guesses[2].

Three types of information structuring could be contemplated. The first is the ordering of tasks within the study itself to ensure an effective progression, but also to understand the interdependencies between tasks to ensure the necessary cross-flow of information. This breakdown typically follows the traditional areas of professional or technical expertise associated with the project domain.

The second structuring is the development of a well-defined, non-overlapping work breakdown of activities for the implementation of the project. Generally these will follow the first structure, but will necessarily contain a greater level of detail, and will include design philosophies, procurement strategies and timing, as well as actual production activities.

The third structuring relates to risk modeling such as a probability/decision tree. This device provides the flexibility for handling different levels of complexity of risk events, including situations requiring complex conditional probability treatment. For each issue considered, the underlying framework for the analysis is a probability tree where each branch represents some combination of potential scenarios and their respective probabilities.

Associated with each scenario will be measures such as economics, delivery and performance impacts. Summarizing the tree will produce overall distributions of project cost, economic return, etc.

The point of structuring the analysis of risks in this way is to enable discussion to focus on specific uncertainties and risks in some level of detail, and provide the basis for establishing the dependency links between the various project activities. It also sets the stage for the subsequent development of schedule network diagrams for the specific analysis of schedule related risks.

2. Risk Identification and Screening

Following the breakdown of the project by activity, the next step is to identify risks associated with each, in order to produce a comprehensive set of uncertainties and risks. The objective is to ensure that all such risks have been considered and discussed, employing judgments from as many relevant sources as possible. In the earliest stages of the project, concern is primarily with fundamental uncertainties, those which could force a change in project scope, or otherwise could be particularly damaging to the success of the project.

At this stage, the classic "brain-storming" approach, concurrent with similar project planning sessions, could be entirely appropriate. However, a more in-depth examination of the compounding effects of seemingly insignificant risks, such as a series of minor delays, can also be very damaging. This is especially true when the project is aimed for a particular "window of opportunity."

Next, all the risks should be coarsely screened to establish those which are:

- Relevant to the project
- Within project responsibility for project management purposes
- Not otherwise covered by normal project insurance
- Predictable (but uncertain)
- More than of minor significance

This should bring the total within manageable proportions. Where several risks have broad implications, they may be conveniently grouped by source as indicated in Appendix A, and further subdivided into discrete events (i.e., single worst cases) and time-scaled events. Care should be exercised to ensure that a risk item judged minor in one case is not major in another.

Once the risks have been assembled and assessed in this way, consideration should be given to joint effects and how these can best be modeled. The level of detail will depend on the study objectives. For example, for the analysis of safety, where complex combinations of low probability risk events and response failures result in accidents, a detailed probability tree which allows conditional probability specification may be necessary. However, for broader study aspects, risks can usually be treated as dependent or independent at some percentage level. This is important to identify, before considering quantification.

3. Risk Quantification

The risks identified in the previous task must now be quantified in terms of degree of uncertainty in a spectrum of certainty/risk/uncertainty (i.e., probability of occurrence) and magnitude of impact (i.e., on project objectives of scope, quality, time and cost). For this purpose, it is necessary to describe the risk together with its primary impact scenario, followed by any consequential impacts. Figure B.1 shows a conceptual relationship between risk probabilities, damage scenarios and consequences.

When estimating impacts, however, it is often necessary to have a set of response decision rules in order to arrive at consistent quantification. This will depend very much on the orientation of the particular project, i.e., whether it is primarily scope, quality, time or cost driven. For example, if a delay is experienced in initiating project realization due to financing delays, will the response be to accept the delay in the interests of quality and cost? Or will steps be taken to accelerate the work by increasing manpower (with the possibility of reduced productivity) in the interests of time?

Such decision rules should be a fundamental part of the basic risk management plan for the project.

More esoteric considerations cover the choice of methods to describe and combine risks for purposes of computation according to standard probability theory. The assumption that all random variables can be described by pre-selected distributions, such as normal distribution, or that all distributions are independent may greatly facilitate calculation, but the results are most likely unreliable. Lack of consideration of the positive dependence that often exists between variables, such as cost and time, may result in serious underestimation.

Perhaps the most contentious aspect of risk analysis is the estimation of probability distribution, due to the scarcity of relevant data. Where available, it may have to be modified to suit the project in question. Where not available, reliance must be placed on totally subjective estimation based on expert opinions and judgments from personal and/or other past experiences (see Delphi Method, Appendix C).

Where insurable risks are concerned, there is a large body of existing knowledge and extensive statistical data on frequency and size of incidents ranging from natural disasters to the man-controlled perils. These data should not be overlooked. Such information is typically available through insurance companies and specialists in risk management.

4. Risk Combination and Modeling

Once the uncertainties and risks have been quantified within each activity of concern, the joint impact of these risks must be considered. Three levels of modeling may need to be examined, namely:

a. The joint impact of a small number of risks for detailed analysis within an activity,

b. The joint effects of all risks within an activity, and

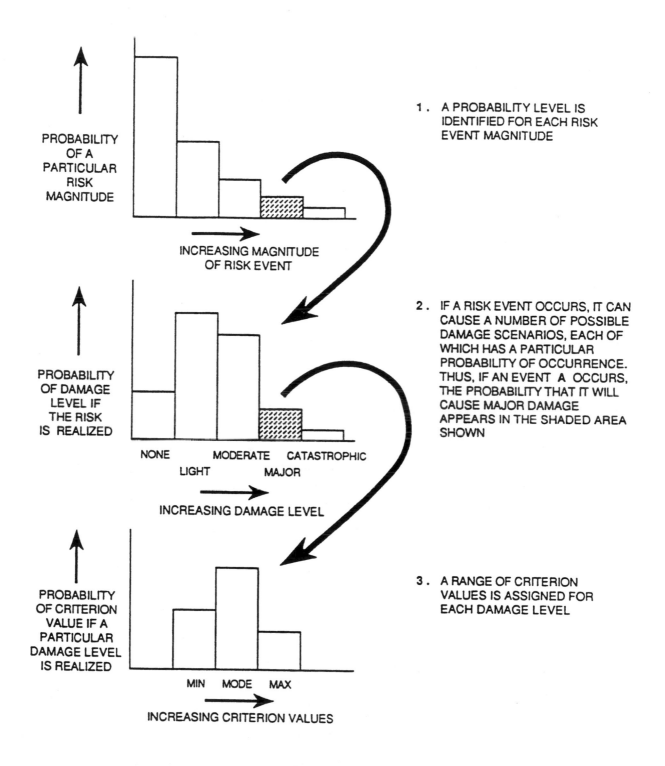

1. A PROBABILITY LEVEL IS IDENTIFIED FOR EACH RISK EVENT MAGNITUDE

2. IF A RISK EVENT OCCURS, IT CAN CAUSE A NUMBER OF POSSIBLE DAMAGE SCENARIOS, EACH OF WHICH HAS A PARTICULAR PROBABILITY OF OCCURRENCE. THUS, IF AN EVENT A OCCURS, THE PROBABILITY THAT IT WILL CAUSE MAJOR DAMAGE APPEARS IN THE SHADED AREA SHOWN

3. A RANGE OF CRITERION VALUES IS ASSIGNED FOR EACH DAMAGE LEVEL

Figure B.1. Conceptual Relationship Between Risks, Damage Scenarios and Consequences
After A.B. Cammaert c. 1986

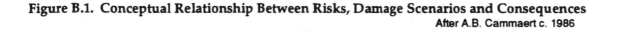

c. The overall impact of risks from a set of, or all, activities.

At each step it is important to review and, if necessary, recycle the results, preferably with the persons responsible within the project team. The purpose is to make team members aware of the uncertainties in the estimates so that inconsistencies and weaknesses in the overall project plan can either be corrected early, or more appropriate courses of action adopted.

As can be seen, these areas of risk quantification and risk modeling can become highly sophisticated. They then become the purview of highly specialized expertise and experience in the particular area of project application.

However, in simpler terms, a criterion value, ranking, or status for each risk event (or set of combined events) may be established by the following relationship:

$$Risk\ Event\ Status\ =\ Risk\ Probability\ x\ Amount\ at\ Stake$$

where probability[3] and the amount-at-stake (i.e., severity) are given by:

$$Probability = \frac{Frequency\ of\ relevant\ events}{Total\ number\ of\ possible\ events}$$

$$Amount\ at\ Stake\ =\ cost\ of\ investment\ loss\ +\ least\ cost\ to\ restore\ status\ quo$$

5. Overall Evaluation

The third level of risk modeling considers the impacts of all risks combined, usually translated into project economics as a common basis. This approach is important since the economic return for a project is determined from the scenarios of project costs, schedules, production, political considerations, and so on, over the whole life of the entity. Nevertheless, considerations of economics alone will not deal with such dimensions as safety and environmental impacts. Depending on the project, these may very well require independent presentation.

6. Project Risk Report

The resulting report should be prepared as a baseline summarizing the findings, changes and/or recommendations, in a form that can be used for subsequent risk response planning, tracking and program updating. Each activity and associated risk events should be clearly described and numbered for reference, along with the impact scenarios envisaged.

Some form of tabulation of the risks considered and their comparative values showing status ranking will be helpful, as well as examples of the major decision trees, and any schedule risk networks developed.

In its simplest form, the expected total value of risks on the project might be presented as a "bottom line" to the project costs as follows:

Project Direct Costs	$ xxx
Project Indirects	$ xx
Interest & other charges	$ xx
etc., etc.	
Expected Value of Risks**	$ xx
TOTAL PROJECT COST	$ xxx

** Note that this may be a more comprehensive and convincing way of expressing an appropriate "contingency" allowance for the project.

A conceptual risk analysis computer program, structured for conducting the type of risk analysis described above, is shown in Figure B.2.

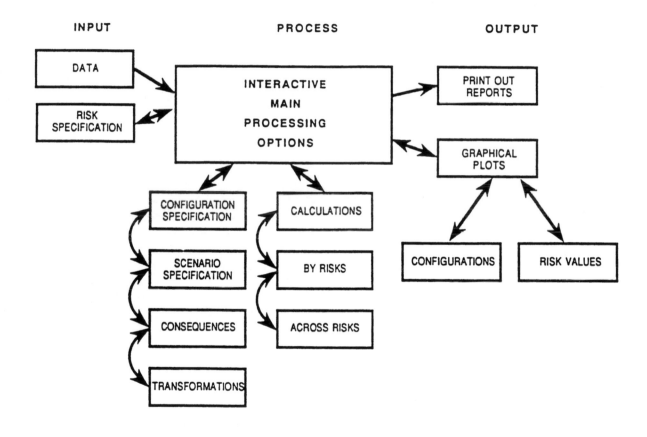

Figure B.2. Simplified Risk Analysis Program Structure

After A.B. Cammaert c. 1986

---

1. Adapted from notes by Dr. A.B. Cammaert, while Manager, Arctic and Off-shore Services, Acres International Limited, Toronto.
2. D.T. Hulett, PMP Certification Workshop - Risk Management, PMI Orange County Chapter, 1991, p3.
3. J.R. Adams, M.D. Martin, A Practical Approach to the Assessment of Project Uncertainty, *PMI Seminar/Symposium Proceedings*, Toronto, 1982, p IV-F.3.

Appendix C

Other Risk Analysis Techniques

Some techniques which can be used to support risk analysis follow. Practical application may be limited to certain types or size of project. Perhaps more important is management's attitude towards risk analysis itself, especially as it tends to be governed more by their understanding of the mathematics involved in the techniques and, consequently, in their confidence in the results produced.

1. Brainstorming

This technique is used extensively in formative project planning, and can also be used to advantage to identify and postulate risk scenarios for a particular project. It is a simple but effective attempt to help people think creatively in a group setting without feeling inhibited or being criticized by others.

A committee is assembled, whose members have as relevant and broad a knowledge of the circumstances of the situation as possible. The rules are that each member must try to build on the ideas offered by preceding comments. No criticism or disapproving verbal or nonverbal behaviors are allowed. The leader or facilitator does not require any special expertise, but must enforce the rules and record the results. The intent is to encourage as many ideas as possible, which may in turn trigger the ideas of others.

In assembling the ideas, any evaluation is strictly reserved for later study. Thus, ideas are encouraged to flow as freely as possible, however imaginative, innovative or wild they may appear. While many suggestions may subsequently be rejected, the greater the number to start with, the more likely that a useful number will be retained, and so provide more comprehensive coverage.

The technique is improved by the variety in the participants' backgrounds and is very helpful in project team building. It is very effective in finding creative solutions to potential problems.

2. Sensitivity Analysis

Sensitivity analysis[1] seeks to place a value on the effect of change of a single variable within a project by analyzing that effect on the project plan. It is the simplest form of risk analysis. Uncertainty and risk are reflected by defining a likely range of variation for each component of the original base case estimate. In practice such an analysis is only done for those variables which have a high impact on cost, time or economic return, and to which the project will be most sensitive.

The effect of change of each of these variables on the final cost or time criteria is then assessed in turn across the assumed ranges. If several variables are changed, the most sensitive or critical variables can be compared graphically in a sensitivity diagram.

Some of the advantages of sensitivity analysis include impressing management that there is a range of possible outcomes, decision making is more realistic, though perhaps more complex, and the relative importance of each variable examined is readily apparent. Some weaknesses are that variables are treated individually, limiting the extent to which combinations of variables can be assessed, and a sensitivity diagram gives no indication of anticipated probability of occurrence.

3. Probability Analysis

Probability analysis[2] overcomes the limitations of sensitivity analysis by specifying a probability distribution for each variable, and then considering situations where any or all of these variables can be changed at the same time. However, since every project is unique, defining the probability of occurrence of any specific variable may be quite difficult, particularly as political or commercial environments can change quite rapidly. Typically, a distribution profile is allocated to the range which has been defined for the variable, and, in the absence of statistical data, simple triangular, trapezoidal or rectangular distributions may be adopted.

As with sensitivity analysis, the range of variation is subjective, but ranges for many time and cost elements of a project estimate should be skewed toward overrun, due to the natural optimism (or omission) of the estimator. The problem of assessing how risks can occur in combination is usually handled by a sampling approach (such as the Monte Carlo technique below) and running the analysis a number of times. The outcome is a range of possible results with their respective probabilities shown diagrammatically, such that reviewers can assess their own attitudes and response to the project and its risks.

4. Delphi Method

The basic concept of the Delphi Method[3] is to derive a consensus using a panel of experts to arrive at a convergent solution to a specific problem. This is particularly useful, for example, in arriving at probability assessments relating to future events where the risk impacts are large and critical. The first and vital step is to select a panel of individuals, as participants, who have experience in the area at issue. For best results the panel members should not know each others identity, and the process should be conducted with each at separate locations. This is to prevent single member influence and simplistic concurrence.

A scenario is established and each panelist is requested to reply to a questionnaire. The responses, together with opinions and justifications, are evaluated and statistical feedback is furnished to each panel member in the next iteration. The process is continued until group responses converge to a specific solution. Should the responses diverge, the facilitator needs to review the wording of the questionnaire, the feedback, or the experience of the panelists to determine if there is a problem which needs to be corrected.

Social scientists are sometimes critical of the method on the grounds that the method has no predictive validity, and that the use of "experts" leads to manipulation of group suggestion rather than consensus.

5. Monte Carlo

The Monte Carlo Method,[4] simulation by means of random numbers, provides a powerful yet simple method of incorporating probabilistic data. The basic steps are:

1. Assess the range for the variables being considered and determine the probability distribution most suited to each.
2. For each variable within its specific range, select a value randomly chosen, taking account of the probability distribution for the occurrence of the variable. This may be achieved by generating the cumulative frequency curve for the variable and choosing a value from a random number table.
3. Run a deterministic analysis using the combination of values selected for each one of the variables.
4. Repeat steps 2 and 3 a number of times to obtain the probability distribution of the result. The number of iterations required depends on the number of variables and the degree of confidence required, but typically lies between 100 and 1000.

6. Decision Tree Analysis

A feature of project work is that a number of options are typically available in the course of reaching the final results. Indeed, even before considering the project in any detail or developing a network analysis for example, the decision maker is faced with an array of procurement possibilities and a sequence of decision choices. The Decision Tree[5] provides a graphical means of bringing the information together. Figure C.1 shows the principle applied to the choice between two projects.

An advantage in its application to risk management is that it forces consideration of the probability of each outcome. Thus, the likelihood of failure is quantified and some value is placed on each decision. This form of risk analysis is usually applied to cost and time considerations, both in choosing between different early investment decisions, and later in considering major changes with uncertain outcomes during project implementation. In the latter case, it may be linked to a sensitivity analysis as a means of determining the value of a certain decision.

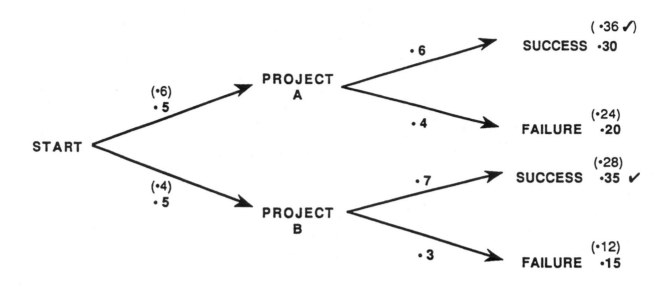

Note the change in recommendation if the initial probability ( ) is changed

Figure C.1. Decision Tree for Two Projects Showing Probabilities Assigned
After J.R. Adams and M.D. Martin, A Practical Approach to the Assessment of Project Uncertainty,
PMI Seminar/Symposium, Toronto, 1982, pIV-F.7

The method is well suited to project risk analysis and has been applied extensively, with additional efforts made to resolve the problem of interrelated risks.

7. Utility Theory

None of the techniques discussed so far take into account the attitude towards risk of the decision maker. It may be reasonable to suppose, for example, that a potential loss of 90 percent would not be viewed with the same equanimity as, say, a loss of 10 percent. Somewhere in between the attitude will change. However, at what point may well depend on the attitude of the decision maker. That is to say, the decision maker may be risk seeking, risk neutral, or risk averse.

Utility Theory[6] endeavors to formalize management's attitude towards risk, an approach which is appropriate to Decision Tree Analysis for the calculation of expected values, and also for the assessment of results from sensitivity and probability analyses. However, in practical project work Utility Theory tends to be viewed as rather theoretical.

8. Decision Theory

Decision Theory[7] is a technique for assisting in reaching decisions under uncertainty and risk. All decisions are based to some extent on uncertain forecasts. Given the criteria selected by the decision maker, Decision Theory points to the best possible course whether or not the forecasts are accurate.

1. J.G. Perry and R.W. Hayes, Risk and its Management in Construction Projects, *Proceedings of the Institute of Civil Engineers*, Part 1, 1985, June 1985.
2. Ibid.
3. M.D. Martin and M.B. McCormick, Improving Project Planning Productivity, *PMI Seminar/Symposium*, Houston, Texas, 1983, p III E5.
4. J.G. Perry and R.W. Hayes, Risk and its Management in Construction Projects, *Proceedings of the Institute of Civil Engineers*, Part 1, 1985, June 1985.
5. Ibid.
6. Ibid.
7. After J.R. Adams and M.D. Martin, A Practical Approach to the Assessment of Project

Appendix D

Risk Applied to Schedule and Cost Analysis

Optimistic-Pessimistic Estimating

It is often possible to describe the likelihood of particular events occurring in such vague terms as quite likely, often, rarely, etc. However, for project purposes it is typically necessary to quantify the probability of an event occurring in order to plan an appropriate response. The use of statistical analysis tools, whether they result in subjective or objective probabilities, enables quantification with some degree of confidence.

For example, in order to develop a realistic project schedule and/or cost, it is necessary to know the durations and/or cost of the various activities involved. When some of those activities are very uncertain, perhaps because they are unfamiliar, a different strategy is required. One estimating strategy which is useful in these circumstances requires making three estimates.

The following approach can be applied to either cost estimating or to time estimating, but for simplicity, the method will be described in the context of scheduling.

The first estimate is an optimistic—corresponding to the shortest possible time if everything falls neatly into place as required. The second estimate is the most likely time—one in which there is a typical balance between things going well and things going poorly. The third estimate is a pessimistic one—the time it will take if difficulties are encountered and a lot of things go wrong. These three estimates can be more technically described as follows:

Optimistic time estimate (o): A time estimate in which a task can be completed if everything goes exceptionally well. An estimate in which the probability of accomplishment is not more than one-in-one hundred (1%), the original PERT assumption.

Most likely time estimate (m): The estimate of the time required for an activity which would be expected to occur most often if the activity could be repeated several times under identical circumstances (without any "learning curve" effects).

Pessimistic time estimate (p): An estimate of the longest time a task might require under the most adverse conditions, barring "acts of God." An estimate in which the probability of not accomplishing the task is less than 1%.

Note that the most-likely-time is a matter of judgement. It is not the same as the "expected time." Expected time (te) is a term given to a calculated weighted average calculated as follows:

Expected Time (t_e): An estimated value calculated from the formula $t_e = (o+4m+p)/6$, where o = optimistic, p = pessimistic and m = most-likely. This relationship is a simplification of the "bell-shaped" curve of probability theory, giving recognition to the fact that such time estimates generally are not symmetrical.

In arriving at the three judgmental estimates, it is desirable to consult with members of the project team who have relevant experience of each activity in question. It will not only lead to establishing better values, but, as a side benefit, involves members of the team and thereby builds commitment to the project plan.

Consider the project plan illustrated below in activity-on-node notation with one time estimate for each activity. Conventional critical path calculations lead to an indicated completion time of 30 days.

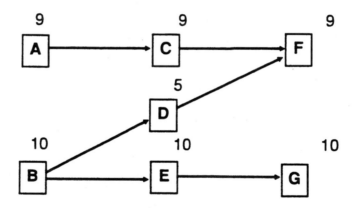

Suppose estimates were obtained for these same activities using the three time estimate approach and the assumptions in the original PERT system. The network and estimates might be as shown below and result in the t_es as shown. Note that these estimates are probably not realistic but are chosen to simplify the illustration and emphasize the a dificiency in conventional PERT.

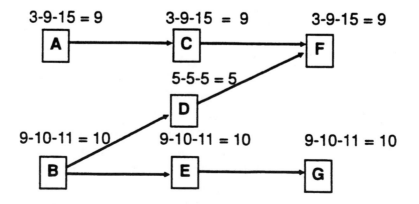

Again, the indicated completion of the project is 30 days but that is now called the "expected completion" of the project. There is a 50% chance of exceeding that time as well as a 50% chance of completing before that time.

Using a concept from probability theory, the Central Limit Theorem, we can combine the uncertainty about the individual activities into an expression of the uncertainty about the project completion time. This requires the calculation of the standard deviations of each activity using the formula, standard deviation = (p - o)/6, per the original PERT concept. Thus, the standard deviations for activities A, C, and F are 2.00 days [(15 - 3)/6] and for activities B, E, and G, 0.33 days [(11 - 9)/6]. For activity D it is, of course, zero.

To get the standard deviation of the completion of the project, the uncertainty of the activities on the critical path must be combined. Theory requires that the standard deviations be "squared" to obtain the "variances" in order to add them so the variances of the activities B, E, and G are 0.111. Adding them gives a variance of .333 of which the "square root," i.e., the standard deviation, is 0.577 days for project completion. This standard deviation can be used with the standard normal distribution to make statements about the probability of completing the project by a specific time. For example, the 95% confidence limits on the normal distribution is based on plus or minus 1.96 standard deviations. Multiplying 1.96 times .577 days gives 1.13 days from which we can say that there is a 95% probability of completing the project in between 28.87 days and 31.13 days. If the target completion date is 31 days, we can state that the probability of being completed by that date is 96%. Thus, the risk of being late or early can be assessed.

This illustration was designed to emphasize a fallacy of the original PERT concept. It assumed that the uncertainty of project completion was dependent only upon the critical path. In this illustration, it can be seen that the second most critical path has a duration of 27 days. However, it is composed of activities which are far more uncertain. They each have standard deviations of 2 days resulting in a standard deviation for the completion of that path being 3.46 days. Thus, the 95% confidence limits for the completion of the project, based on this path, are 20.22 days to 33.78 days and the probability of project completion in 31 days is now only 88%. This path has greater potential of causing a delay in project completion than the critical path and therefore poses greater risk.

A solution to this anomaly exists however, in project management software which incorporates a Monte Carlo Simulation approach to analyzing uncertainty. This approach is identical to the above up to the point of calculating the project completion time. Instead of using the expected times (t_e), a procedure is used which takes samples from the range of durations for each activity using random numbers. Thus, in any given calculation, one activity may have a performance time near its optimistic, another near its pessimistic, and another near its most likely, and so forth. The frequency of selection of times within this range is consistent with the probability distribution of durations for each activity. The resulting completion time from that calculation is then an observation in the development of the distribution of completion times for the project completion and is a function of the uncertainty of every activity in the project.

This resulting distribution is then a reasonably accurate reflection of the uncertainty associated with the completion of the project and can be used effectively in risk analysis of project completion times.

There have been several variations developed from the original PERT. One of those, by Moder[1], argues that the optimistic and pessimistic time estimates are more likely to be a reflection of one-in-twenty occurences than one-in-one hundred. If that is true, then the divisor for the standard deviation is 3.2. Otherwise the calculations and concepts are the same.

Impact Analysis: Probability of Event and Severity of Consequences

The relationship between probability and severity of consequences is shown schematically in Figure D.1.

Event probabilities can often be estimated using statistical inferences based on history. Severity of consequences may be similarly derived or by estimating the impact of specific events by

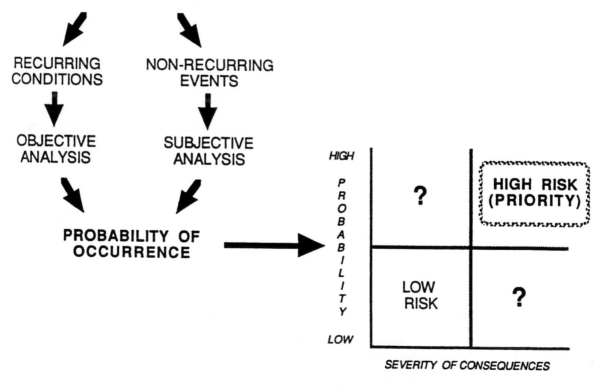

Figure D.1.

developing resulting scenarios. Expected Value (EV) can be used to adjust the value of the consequences of any given outcome for the probability of its occurence.

Assume that our project has an estimated cost of $90,000 and has to be completed in 31 days. In addition, there is a $50,000 penalty if completion takes longer. How significant is this risk?

In our schedule example described earlier, based on the most risky path there was an 88% chance of completing the project in 31 days or less; therefore, there is a 12% chance that the project would not be completed in 31 days. The expected cost is calculated as the sum of the products of the value of an outcome times the probability that that outcome will occur as follows.

Outcome	Value of the Outcome		Probability		Product
Complete in 31 days or less	$90,000	x	.88	=	$79,200
Complete in more than 31 days	140,000	x	.12	=	16,800
			Expected Value	=	$96,000

From this calculation it will be seen that the EV of the cost is substantially higher than the estimated cost and the calculation provides a clearer basis for management decision as, for example, a decision as to whether or not to invest in an R&D project.

The calculation also provides a basis for other comparative calculations. For instance, whether or not a schedule slippage beyond the 31 day point is a high risk or a low one depends on the consequences that may result. In real-world terms, it may also depend on who is responsible for the slippage.

Consider the "normal" experience that design changes cause schedule slippages. Suppose that our experience of the type of project calculated earlier shows that there is a 50/50 chance of the project's client requesting a design change, and further that according to our records client-ordered changes have led to a delay on 70% of the occasions. Then, if a schedule slippage occurs on this project, what is the likelihood that it will be caused by a client-ordered design change? This calculation is shown below:

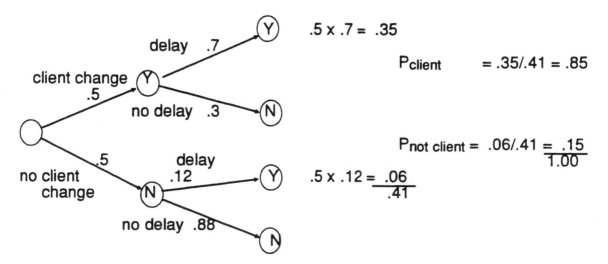

$$.5 \times .7 = .35$$

$$P_{client} = .35/.41 = .85$$

$$P_{not\ client} = .06/.41 = \frac{.15}{1.00}$$

$$.5 \times .12 = \frac{.06}{.41}$$

The results show that there is an 85% chance of the responsibility being with the client, and therefore a 15% chance that the slippage will <u>not</u> be due to the client. The calculation of the revised EV of cost is shown as $90,900.

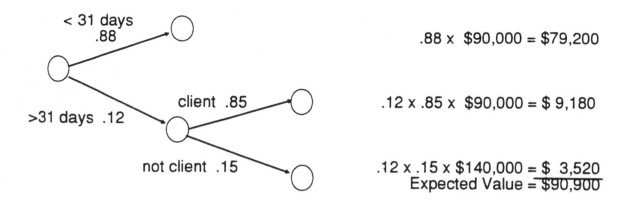

.88 x $90,000 = $79,200

.12 x .85 x $90,000 = $ 9,180

.12 x .15 x $140,000 = $ 3,520
Expected Value = $90,900

Taking into account that there is only a 12% chance of over-running the 31 day limit and only a 15% chance of the penalty being imposed, and that these two events are assumed to be independent, then the probability of incurring the $50,000 late completion penalty is about 2% (12% x 15%). Conversely, the probability of there being no penalty, even if the project is late, is 98%.

REVENUE   less   EXPECTED COST   = EV PROFIT

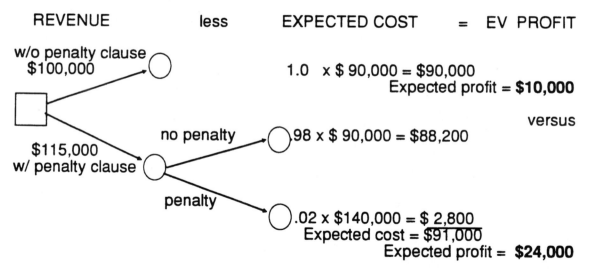

1.0   x $ 90,000 = $90,000
Expected profit = **$10,000**

versus

.98 x $ 90,000 = $88,200

.02 x $140,000 = $ 2,800
Expected cost = $91,000
Expected profit = **$24,000**

Consider the possibility of having a choice between taking on the project at a Firm Fixed Price (FFP) of $115,000 with the penalty clause, or at $100,000 without the penalty clause. Which option should be taken?

An aid to answering this question can be obtained by using the above probabilities to compare the two alternatives, FFP without penalty clause and FFP with penalty clause.

The probability calculation shows that the EV of the profit from a FFP of $100,000 with no penalty is $10,000. This does not consider any increase in costs due to the project exceeding the expected completion time of 30 days (derived from the original PERT calculations) or savings from completing in less than 30 days, outcomes which each have a probability of 50%. The EV of the profit from a FFP of $115,000, with penalty, is $24,000. A risk taker could be expected to take the second option as the EV of profit is greater. In other words, there is a 98% probability of a $25,000 profit even when offset by an 2% chance of a $25,000 loss. This could be considered a better deal than a $10,000 profit guaranteed.

Note, however, that expected value theory assumes that the risk taker is playing this game a large number of times and that in any single play the risk taker can afford to take the loss, should it occur.

Guidelines for Use of Expected Value Techniques

1. The risk assessment process should not be started with a preconceived point of view.

2. Keep an open mind until an objective decision has been reached.

3. Ensure objectivity in defining the risk, reward and remedy and in the data collection process.

4. Avoid biased subjective probability judgements and accurately estimate the value of the reward and the cost of the potential remedial action.

5. If the probabilities are defined by a range of values, use the conservative end of the range in the analysis.

6. If the computed expected value of profit is clearly negative, DON'T TAKE THE RISK, if that is an option.

7. If the computed expected value of profit is clearly positive, TAKE THE RISK, provided the loss can be afforded, should it occur.

8. If the sign (positive) of the computed expected value of profits can change with slight adjustments in the probability judgements or in the estimated reward or remedy, DON'T TAKE THE RISK.

9. If there are any doubts at all about the situation (risk, reward, remedy or probabilities of success and failure), DON'T TAKE THE RISK.

10. Once the risk has been taken, be ready to implement a contingency plan if and when it is realized that the desired outcome cannot be achieved.

---

1. Moder, Joseph J., Cecil R. Phillips, and Edward W. Davis. 1983. *Project Management With CPM, PERT and Precedence Diagramming*. Third Edition. p. 283. Van Nostrand Reinhold Company: New York.

Appendix E

A Glossary of Project and Program Risk Management Terminology

Note: The project and program risk management context is implicit throughout the following definitions.

Activities. A series of tasks performed over a period of time.

Amount at Stake. The extent of adverse consequences which could occur to the project.

Business Risk. The inherent chances for both profit or loss associated with a particular endeavor.

Contingency Allowance. Specific provision to cover variations which may occur in the expected values of elements of cost or schedule, but not scope or quality (see Contingency Reserve).

Contingency Planning. The development of management plans to be invoked in the event of specified *risk events*. Examples include the provision and prudent management of a *contingency allowance* in the budget, the preparation of alternative schedule activity sequences, *work-arounds* and emergency responses to reduce the impacts of particular *risk events*, and the evaluation of liabilities in the event of complete project shut down.

Contingency Reserve. A provision held by the project sponsor for possible changes in project scope or quality. Scope and quality changes constitute changes in the project manager's mandate and will affect the project's cost and schedule (see Contingency Allowance).

Control. Planning, monitoring accomplishment, and exercising any necessary corrective action to yield the required outcome.

Deflection. The act of transferring all or part of a *risk* to another party, usually by some form of contract.

Go/No-Go Decision. A major decision point in the project life cycle, typically marking the transition from planning to accomplishment.

Historical Database. Records accumulating past project experience stored as data for use in estimating, forecasting and predicting future events.

Insurable Risk. A particular type of risk which can be covered by an insurance policy.

Impact Analysis. The mathematical examination of the nature of individual risks on the project, as well as potential arrangements of interdependent risks. It includes the quantification of their respective impact severity, probability, and sensitivity to changes in related project variables, including the project life cycle. To be complete, the analysis should also include an examination of the external "status quo" prior to project implementation as well as the project's internal intrinsic worth as a reference baseline. A determination should also be made as to whether all risks identified are within the scope of the project's *response planning* process.

Known, Known-Unknown, Unknown-Unknown. A method of classifying risks according to the amount of information available.

Mitigation. The act of revising the project's scope, budget, schedule or quality, preferably without material impact on the project's objectives, in order to reduce *uncertainty* on the project.

Opportunity. The cumulative effect of the chances of uncertain occurrences which will affect project objectives positively. Opportunity is the opposite of *risk*.

Post-Project Review. An appraisal of all aspects of a project upon completion, with a view to examining and documenting variations and events, to augment the organization's historical database.

Probability. The likelihood of occurrence. The ratio of the number of chances by which an event may happen (or not happen) to the sum of the chances of both happening and not happening.

Process. The set of activities required to achieve an output.

Pure Risk. See insurable risk.

Public Relations. An activity designed to improve the environment in which a project organization operates in order to improve project performance and reception.

Response Planning. The process of formulating suitable *risk management* strategies for the project, including the allocation of responsibility to the project's various functional areas. It may involve *mitigation*, *deflection* and *contingency planning*. Some flexibility should also be provided, however tentative, for the completely unforeseen occurrence.

Risk (Project Risk). The cumulative effect of the chances of an uncertain occurrences which will adversely affect project objectives. It is the degree of exposure to negative events and their probable consequences. Project *risk* is characterized by three *risk factors*: *risk event*, *risk probability* and the *amount at stake*. Risk is the opposite of *opportunity*.

Risk Data Applications. The development of a database of *risk factors*, actual responses and consequences, both for the current project and as a matter of historic record.

Risk Event. The precise description of what might happen to the detriment of the project.

Risk Event Status. A measure of importance of a *risk event*. Also referred to as criterion value or simply its ranking.

Risk Factor. Any one of *risk event, risk probability* or *amount at stake.*

Risk Identification. The process of systematically identifying all possible *risk events* which may impact on a project. They may be conveniently classified according to their cause or source and ranked roughly according to ability to manage effective responses. Not all risk events will impact all projects, but the cumulative effect of several risk events occurring in conjunction may well be more severe than examination of individual risk events might suggest.

Risk Management. The art and science of identifying, analyzing and responding to *risk factors* throughout the life of a project and in the best interests of its objectives.

Risk Probability. The degree to which the *risk event* is likely to occur.

Risk Response System. The ongoing process put in place during the life of the project to monitor, review and update *project risk* and make the necessary adjustments. Examination of the various *risks* will show that some risks are greater in some stages of the project life cycle than in others.

Success (Project Success). The achievement of stakeholder satisfaction.

Surprise. The surfacing of an unanticipated *uncertainty,* either *opportunity* or *risk event.*

Technique. Skilled means to an end.

Total Certainty. All information is known.

Total Uncertainty. No information is available and nothing is known. By definition, total uncertainty cannot be envisaged.

Uncertainty. The possibility that events may occur which will impact the project either favorably or unfavorably. Uncertainty gives rise to both *opportunity* and *risk.*

Work-around. An alternative solution to a potential problem.

YOUR COMMENTS
on
Project and Program Risk Management

HELP US HELP YOU!

So that we may better provide you with the practical information you need, please take a moment to record your comments on this page and return it to:

The Executive Director
Project Management Institute
130 South State Road
Upper Darby, PA 19082
U.S.A.

I/we have the following suggestions regarding this handbook:_____

_____

_____

_____

_____

_____

_____

_____

_____

_____

_____

_____

_____

_____

_____

_____

_____

_____

_____

Name_____

Address_____

City_____State_____ZIP Code_____

Country_____Date_____

R. Max Wideman, *P.Eng. FEIC, FICE, Fellow PMI, is a professional engineer specializing in project management consulting. Since graduating at London University, his experience has included hydroelectric, river, marine, transportation, industrial, institutional, commercial and residential projects. He has also been instrumental in social and environmental impact studies, major contract and expropriation claims, construction productivity, and project management audit. In working for a diversity of sectors, he has gained a broad perspective and insight into the project management process.*

Mr. Wideman has lectured extensively, presenting papers or seminars on a variety of project management topics in Canada, China, Egypt, Iceland, India, Jamaica, Pakistan, the Philippines, Saudi Arabia, the United Kingdom, and the USA.

In 1974, Mr. Wideman joined the Project Management Institute (PMI) and later launched the PMI West Coast BC chapter. In 1982 he was elected to the International Board as Vice President Member Services and served as director for three years. During this time, he was assigned responsibility for expanding and codifying PMI's existing standards of knowledge by conducting a major voluntary study by PMI members. The resulting report became known as the Project Management Body of Knowledge, or "PMBOK," which was approved by the PMI Board in March 1987.

Mr. Wideman received PMI's Distinguished Contribution to Project Management Award in 1985, and the following year was honored as PMI Person-of-the-Year. He was elected PMI president for 1987, became chairman in 1988, and was made a Fellow of the Institute in 1989. Mr. Wideman has authored a number of articles and papers for the Institute's publications and is author of Cost Control of Capital Projects, AEW Services, Vancouver, 1983.

Code of Ethics
for
The Project Management Profession

PREAMBLE: Project Management Professionals, in the pursuit of the profession, affect the quality of life for all people in our society. Therefore, it is vital that Project Management Professionals conduct their work in an ethical manner to earn and maintain the confidence of team members, colleagues, employees, employers, clients and the public.

ARTICLE I: Project Management Professionals shall maintain high standards of personal and professional conduct, and:

a. Accept responsibility for their actions.

b. Undertake projects and accept responsibility only if qualified by training or experience, or after full disclosure to their employers or clients of pertinent qualifications.

c. Maintain their professional skills at the state of the art and recognize the importance of continued personal development and education.

d. Advance the integrity and prestige of the profession by practicing in a dignified manner.

e. Support this code and encourage colleagues and co-workers to act in accordance with this code.

f. Support the professional society by actively participating and encouraging colleagues and co-workers to participate.

g. Obey the laws of the country in which work is being performed.

ARTICLE II: Project Management Professionals shall, in their work:

a. Provide the necessary project leadership to promote maximum productivity while striving to minimize costs.

b. Apply state of the art project management tools and techniques to ensure quality, cost and time objectives, as set forth in the project plan, are met.

c. Treat fairly all project team members, colleagues and co-workers, regardless of race, religion, sex, age or national origin.

d. Protect project team members from physical and mental harm.

e. Provide suitable working conditions and opportunities for project team members.

f. Seek, accept and offer honest criticism of work, and properly credit the contribution of others.

g. Assist project team members, colleagues and co-workers in their professional development.

ARTICLE III: Project Management Professionals shall, in their relations with employers and clients:

a. Act as faithful agents or trustees for their employers and clients in professional or business matters.

b. Keep information on the business affairs or technical processes of an employer or client in confidence while employed, and later, until such information is properly released.

c. Inform their employers, clients, professional societies or public agencies of which they are members or to which they may make any presentations, of any circumstance that could lead to a conflict of interest.

d. Neither give nor accept, directly or indirectly, any gift, payment or service of more than nominal value to or from those having business relationships with their employers or clients.

e. Be honest and realistic in reporting project quality, cost and time.

ARTICLE IV: Project Management Professionals shall, in fulfilling their responsibilities to the community:

a. Protect the safety, health and welfare of the public and speak out against abuses in these areas affecting the public interest.

b. Seek to extend public knowledge and appreciation of the project management profession and its achievements.